Volume One

Angels At War

Secrets of Spiritual Warfare Revealed

Sharon M. Cluck

Published BY: Mind of Messiah Ministries

What People are Saying

If you have ever wondered if angels surround you, this book will strengthen your faith and supercharge your walk with God. Did you know that angels have been watching over us since birth, accompanying us wherever we venture? Writes author Sharon Cluck, "They are with you the moment you call out to God." Whether we see them or not, they are working on our behalf as God directs, giving them their marching orders in service to humanity. Angels at War! Secrets of Spiritual Warfare Revealed is a treasure trove of wisdom, inspiration, and insight into the angelic realm. Replete with Scriptural references, as well as Compelling personal encounters, this book will be hard for readers to put down. The "secrets" of spiritual warfare are really "hidden in plain sight" throughout the Bible, and Sharon has the ability to bring them to light through her teaching and storytelling. If you want to understand the supernatural nature of our mortal existence, our relationship to the angels as fellow servants of the Most High God, and the plan He has for His heavenly and earthly families to advance His Kingdom, Angels at War! Secrets of Spiritual Warfare Revealed is a must-read for every follower of Jesus the Messiah.

Tracy Tennant
Author, speaker, podcaster
Founder, Equipping Christians Ministries

Spiritual warfare, though often misunderstood, is a fundamental reality for anyone committed to a life of faith and righteousness. From the very first pages of Angels at War, I quickly found myself immersed in the depths of the principles of spiritual warfare- shedding light on strategies and divine truths that will enable believers to stand firm against spiritual adversaries. Sharon does an outstanding job of introducing biblical principles along with real-life, personal experiences that allow the reader to fully understand what she is communicating, equipping the reader with the tools for victory over the forces of darkness that seek to undermine faith, hope, and love in their lives. As Christ's followers, we not only have a right but a true responsibility to grow in our spiritual knowledge. Our hunger for spiritual enlightenment must be reignited! As you journey through the pages, you will be challenged to reconsider how you view your daily struggles, recognizing that life's challenges are not merely isolated incidents. Still, they are often manifestations of a greater, unseen war. Sharon's book is a true feast on God's Word and confirms His desire to intervene on our behalf through His warring angels. This book displays her vast knowledge of scriptures, real-life accounts, and personal victories of spiritual triumph, which allows the reader to be empowered to confront and overcome these forces in their own lives through strength and faith.

I had a hard time putting this book down and I appreciate the time and biblical research that had to take place to share this revelation of angels with those of us who desire to know more of God's principles. I believe that those who read its words will have their eyes opened and their hearts enlightened to truly see the angelic presence that is provided to help us-a gift from our Heavenly Father. Your spiritual knowledge will definitely be enhanced as you engage with the material written in Angels at War!

Pastor Sherry Polete
Praise Temple, Fredericktown, MO.

I truly enjoyed "Angels at War." Each chapter was filled with new secrets about spiritual warfare, and it just kept getting better. It's an excellent resource for teaching the Church about the awareness of angels and their role in our daily battles. This book shows us how angels are continually revealing things to us. Sharon offers valuable insights into what the Church needs to learn in this area. We aren't paying enough attention to these powerful beings or the roles they play in the scriptures and in our personal lives every day. Angels are powerful forces who are fighting alongside us, yet we remain unaware of their assistance. I believe everyone in the ministry should be reading this book.

Senior Pastor Gene Rauls
Praise Temple Church

Copyright 2025 by Sharon M. Cluck
www.mindofmessiah.com
Mind of Messiah Publishing, 5131 Bonney Lane, Farmington, Mo. 63640. All rights reserved. You may use brief quotations from this resource in presentations, articles, and books. Otherwise, no part of this publication may be reproduced, stored in a retrieval system, or transmitted in any form or by any means, electronic, mechanical, photocopy, recording, scanning, or any other without the prior permission of Mind of Messiah Publishing.

Unless otherwise noted, Scripture quotations are from the King James Version (KJV)

"Scripture quotations taken from The Holy Bible, New International Version® NIV® Copyright © 1973, 1978, 1984, 2011 by Biblica, Inc. Used with permission. All rights reserved worldwide."

"Scripture quotations taken from the Amplified® Bible (AMP), Copyright © 1954, 1958, 1962, 1964, 1965, 1987 by The Lockman Foundation. Used by permission. All rights reserved. www.Lockman.org"

Scripture quotations marked TPT are from The Passion Translation®. Copyright © 2017, 2018, 2020 by Passion & Fire Ministries, Inc. Used by permission. All rights reserved. ThePassionTranslation.com.

Scripture quotations marked (CJB) are taken from the COMPLETE JEWISH BIBLE, copyright© 1998 by David H. Stern. Published by Jewish New Testament Publications, Inc. www.messianicjewish.net/ jntp. Distributed by Messianic Jewish Resources Int'l. www.messianicjewish.net. All rights reserved. Used by permission.

In Scripture quotations, the author added emphasis in boldface, and it was not part of the original translation.

ISBN 978-1-7350660-1-1

Contents

Introduction 8
Angels and Spiritual Warfare 8

Chapter One. 17
My First Spiritual Warfare Encounter! 17

Chapter Two 29
What IS Spiritual Warfare? 29

Chapter 3. 50
Jacob's Angelic Rescue 50

Chapter 4. 63
Angels Respond to Our Words! 63

Chapter 5. 80
It's a War of Words! 80

Chapter 6. 96
Yahweh Sabaoth (Lord of Host) 96

Chapter 7. 114
Angels to the Rescue! 114

Chapter 8. 130
Our Miracle Working God! 130

Chapter 9. 144
A Redeemer in Israel! 144

Chapter 10. 159
The Breakout Angel! 159

Chapter 11 165
The Divine Counsel 165
Chapter 12 187
The Decree of The Watchers! 187
Chapter 13 210
Joshua 210
Bibliography 233
Secrets by Chapter: 234

Introduction

Angels and Spiritual Warfare

You are about to discover secrets related to spiritual warfare and the strength of angelic assistance that you likely have not encountered before.

This book was intended to focus mainly on angels who wage war on behalf of God's people. However, our home group had been meeting for prayer when several of those attending experienced encounters with angels. I, too, had seen and heard angels on many occasions. Wanting to support those experiences with the Word of God, we embarked on this study. As I researched, it was apparent that angels were integrally involved in spiritual warfare alongside mankind. The original intent was to call this book "Angels That War," with no subtitle.

That's when I was awakened in the night with a voice that said, "Sharon, these are SECRETS! Sharon, these are Secrets! The Lord continued, "Many are completely unaware of this information. I want you to call the book "Angels That War, Secrets of Spiritual Warfare!"

There are two kingdoms at work on Earth: The Kingdom of God, which is light, and the Kingdom of Darkness, ruled by the fallen angel, whom we refer to as the devil or Satan. Both operate simultaneously. If we don't recognize this, we will be deceived, believing that what is good is evil and what is evil is good. I have heard it said that John 10:10 is the dividing line of the entire Bible. I had trouble comprehending this at first.

> *The thief comes only in order to steal and kill and destroy. I came that they may have and enjoy life, and have it in abundance [to the full, till it overflows]. Jn. 10:10 Amp.*

I didn't understand how something in the New Testament could be called the dividing line of the Bible until I realized that from the beginning of Genesis to the end of Revelation, there is a battle between good and evil. Therefore, we can assess everything in the Bible and in life by identifying which Kingdom is initiating any action. You can understand who or what is the driving force behind everything we see or hear. Ask yourself: does this bring life, or does it lead to death?

We desperately need the spirit of discernment to understand what is behind the forces in our world today. If we are discerning, we will be able to identify the Kingdom behind every action we witness.

You and I are caught in the middle of this battle between kingdoms. We live in a war zone without realizing it. When we finally awaken to the reality of this conflict, having angels fighting alongside us will provide great confidence. They are present in both major and minor confrontations alike. They are an essential asset to our daily individual struggles, just as they were for the characters within the pages of Scripture. We have overlooked just how involved they are and how much they love to assist those in the Kingdom of God.

The Father desires for all of us to be well-equipped spiritually for the end of days. Many signs indicate that those days are upon us now. God has a remnant; they are a powerful group of believers who will stand with Him until the end. We are known as "Overcomers." We are alive at this crucial time in history to put our foot on hell and to enforce the victory that Yeshua/Jesus has already won.

The battle becomes much easier when you know you're not alone. I began to research and reflect on how angels supported the everyday events of believers in God's Word. What kinds of challenges did they face daily? Many answers to these questions are revealed within the pages of this book.

Most believers have no problem accepting that the prophets and the disciples had angelic interactions. However, when it comes to their own daily battles, they doubt that the angels will manifest on their behalf.

If you journey through these pages to the end, you will be much better prepared to face whatever challenges come your way in the difficult times ahead. As we revisit familiar Bible stories, I'm confident you will see them from a fresh perspective. You'll say, "Well, I never saw it that way before!"

My prayer for you is to hear the voice of the Father. May your heart leap with excitement at the prospect of a constant angelic presence in your own life. I pray you have an open mind and heart to begin seeing the unseen in this earthly realm. Know that we are never alone, and our weapons are mighty for pulling down strongholds. You are never expected to face the enemy unescorted. The Bible tells us we have spiritual eyes and spiritual ears. All we need to do is learn to open them.

> *The weapons we fight with are not the weapons of this world. On the contrary, they have divine power to demolish strongholds. 2 Cor. 10:4 NIV*

It is essential to remember that our focus in Spiritual Warfare is not on the size of the enemy but on the greatness and power of our God. I'm grateful that you and I are part of the family of God, which includes His faithful angelic forces. We may not always see them, but I am fully convinced that they are present. We have the authority to use Jesus/Yeshua's name, which empowers us to walk in His strength, causing demons to tremble and flee. Our weapons, which include angelic armies, are so powerful that they demolish strongholds.

The church, in general, has not made it a practice to teach God's people about Spiritual Warfare. If anything, they may have only been given a general understanding of the "Armor of God." One thing I am sure of is that the body lacks understanding of who battles alongside us. That topic has been entirely neglected.

We don't just have one or two angels; we always have an entire army of angelic support available to us. Some of us see them, while others do not. Believe me, they are there 24/7. We don't have to see to believe. If you are reading this, I trust that you are a person of faith.

Secret: The wounds of your past blur your Spiritual Vision.

Through years of training and experience, I have come to know and understand, without a doubt, that we are all wounded in one way or another. We can't get through this life without something causing emotional scars. Because of that wounding, most of us have established a self-protective mechanism. We build up walls. Those walls prevent us from intimacy, not only with humanity but also with God, the creator of the universe.

I've learned that as a person heals from childhood and lifelong wounds, the walls and protective mechanisms begin to crumble. As this happens, our understanding starts to open to the truths of the Word of God. It's a crucial key to perceiving the supernatural world.

We start to see with spiritual eyes, perceiving things we weren't capable of before. Our spiritually blind eyes become enlightened. The amount of emotional and spiritual healing a person experiences is usually directly related to their ability to see and hear in the spirit.

Some form of inner healing is necessary for almost everyone. It starts with seeking God's face. Begin by asking Him to reveal any unforgiveness you might be holding onto. That's the first step in breaking down the walls you've built up.

Wounds and barriers are a topic for another book. However, this is your heads-up if you're wondering why you don't see with spiritual eyes. You have likely been hurt and are hesitant to trust in the unseen.

Hopefully, you have heard something about the weapons of our warfare. It's concerning how many Christians don't realize they are in a war. So, let's revisit this verse.

> *For the weapons of our warfare are not carnal, but mighty through God to the pulling down of strong holds. 2 Cor 10:4*

I could hang out here and talk about strongholds, which are important but not the focus of this book. One of the greatest weapons in our warfare arsenal is an amazing "Army of Angels" at our disposal. They are already trained for battle. These warriors are beyond our belief. Equipped with unimaginable weaponry, the enemy has nothing that compares to the advanced arms of these magnificent beings who are ever ready and willing to fight for you and me.

Your confidence and boldness grow extraordinarily when you begin to see and hear in the spirit. Until then, we sometimes need to be reminded that only one-third of the angels fell or rebelled against God. There is truly more with us than against us. I feel privileged to have witnessed some of these armies. I hope you will experience the supernatural in your life before you finish this book. Once you become aware of it, you are more likely to recognize it when it appears.

Nothing in the Word prohibits God from creating additional angels after one-third fell. Have you ever thought about that? He certainly has the ability, and nothing is impossible with God.

This verse supports the idea that a third of the angels fell, and it's the only one I know of. Furthermore, how can we be sure it's being interpreted correctly? It's the sole reference that mentions a third of the stars falling. Therefore, it's not entirely clear that we have this right.

> *And his tail drew the third part of the stars of heaven, and did cast them to the earth: Rev. 12:4a*

He is referring to Satan, and the term "stars" typically refers to angels in the scriptures.

Secret: God has Two Families.

Most people have never considered the fact that God has two families: * one on earth that we can see—that's us, humankind—and another that moves between the earth and the third heaven, the angels. God originally intended us to be one big happy family until Adam fell. Both angels and humans are created beings by the same creator. The angels faithful to God's throne love us just as the Father loves us. Have you ever thought about angels loving you or caring about what's happening in your life? After all, they rejoiced over us when humankind was created. They were there watching, which is clear when God asked Job where he was when the earth was created.

> *Where wast thou when I laid the foundations of the earth? declare, if thou hast understanding. Who hath laid the measures thereof, if thou knowest? or who hath stretched the line upon it? Whereupon are the foundations thereof fastened? or who laid the corner stone thereof; When the morning stars sang together, and all the sons of God shouted for joy? Job 38:4-7*

Morning stars and sons of God are the angels. You and I are seen in this earthly realm while they remain mostly unseen to us. The creator of the angels is the same God who formed Adam and Eve. Because humankind inherited Adam's sinful nature, a veil has been placed between the two families. This veil prevents us from seeing beyond our earthly realm unless we are granted that privilege through our intimacy with Yeshua/Jesus.

When we receive our glorified bodies, the veil will be lifted, and we will see clearly. The family will be reunited again.

* Michael Heiser, "Unseen Realm," "Angels."

> *For now we see through a glass, darkly; but then face to face: now I know in part; but then shall I know even as also I am known. 1 Co. 13:12*

Do you think God knows you? He knows everything about you. When that veil is lifted, we will know and be known just as God knows us. In the book of Hebrews, we discover that angels are spirits who serve. Much like us, they are servants of the Most High God.

> *Moreover, to which of the angels has he ever said, "Sit at my right hand until I make your enemies a footstool for your feet"? Heb. 1:13*

He has never said this to any angel, including Satan who was originally an angel. When I read this, I can almost hear God saying, "Certainly not YOU, devil." The earth is not your footstool." It is the Lord's, and all that is in it.

> *Are they not all ministering spirits, sent forth to minister for them who shall be heirs of salvation? KJV Heb. 1:14*

That's us. We are the ones God delivers, and His faithful angels are always present to assist us. You are a spirit; you have a soul, and you live in a body. When you enter the kingdom of God (becoming born again), you are a spirit serving the King, just like the angels do. That's what the Bible states. Aren't they all spirits who serve? Sent out to minister to us, the heirs of salvation.

So, we are the ones whom God is delivering. You and I are the heirs of salvation, and the angels loyal to God's throne are always present to assist us. They are fellow servants of God, serving with us.

> *And he said unto me, These sayings are faithful and true: and the Lord God of the holy prophets sent his angel to shew unto his servants the things which must shortly be done. Behold, I come quickly: blessed is he that keepeth the sayings of the prophecy of*

*this book. And I John saw these things, and heard them. And when I had heard and seen, I fell down to worship before the feet of the angel which shewed me these things. Then saith he unto me, See thou do it not: for I am thy **fellowservant**, and **of thy brethren the prophets**, and of them which keep the sayings of this book: worship God. Rev. 22:6-9*

The term "fellow servant" in Greek refers to being a co-slave, a minister of the same master (whether human or divine). As a family, we share the same purpose (human or angelic) to serve our Master as one. We are all created to be united with the Father.

The angels are sent to reveal things to us—things that are yet to come. They are fellow servants alongside us, the prophets, and those who uphold the teachings of THE Book! They reveal things to us to come.

While journaling one day, God revealed to me that Roe v. Wade would be overturned by the Supreme Court. It was two years before it happened. I recorded it in my journal and only shared it with a few other believers. I didn't trust that I had heard God correctly. I prayed for this for 40 years. Under the new administration that had just taken office in our U.S. Capital, it seemed impossible. They were strictly pro-abortion. But God knew and revealed it long before it occurred.

Even though I couldn't comprehend how it would be possible, it happened just as it had been revealed. God knew I had almost given up on it ever becoming a reality. Because God is greater and more powerful than any political party or administration that governs this earth, He can accomplish far more than we ever give Him credit for. He is truly an amazing God.

In the above scripture, the angel tells John that they are his fellow servants. They are also fellow servants of the prophets and fellow servants of those who keep the sayings of this book.

The angel said, "I am your servant, and I also serve the prophets." Do you get that?

If you are among those who uphold the teachings of the book, specifically the book of Revelation, then you share a purpose with the angels. Take a moment to reflect on that. In the church, we refer to each other as brother and sister, but do we view the angels as our brothers or even as fellow servants?

In the world, if two people have the same father, they are considered brothers. God is the creator of the angel family, just as He is the creator of the human family on earth. The difference is that we are created in the image of God Himself, with the ability to function in an earthly environment. At the same time, angels are designed to operate in both heavenly and earthly realms. We'll explore more about this in the following chapters.

The scriptures tell us that we are seated in heavenly places with Christ Jesus. Perhaps we, too, are able to operate in both realms, but we just haven't learned how to yet!

Secret: We can be in two places at once.

> *He hath raised us up together, and made us sit together in heavenly places in Christ Jesus: Eph. 2:6*

Angels often travel between heaven and earth. The Apostle Paul mentioned knowing a man who ascended to the third heaven, indicating that it is indeed possible for a human to access both heaven and earth.

Chapter One.

My First Spiritual Warfare Encounter!

Secret: Unseen Spirits can apply physical force in this realm.

Before we proceed, I'd like to share a bit of my own journey. Who am I, and how did I learn about "Spiritual Warfare?"

I've been involved with the deliverance ministry since 1975 and have taught spiritual warfare for decades. In 2005, I began to see truths in the Word that changed my life forever. Consequently, I started observing a Saturday Sabbath, reflecting on what I saw Jesus doing in the scriptures. This practice has been a part of my spiritual growth. My encounters with the supernatural have increased as I've learned to walk in greater obedience. I desired my walk to mirror that of Jesus/Yeshua. Whatever I saw Him do, I aimed to do as well. If He didn't participate in certain activities, I chose to refrain from those, such as worldly traditions and holidays. I wanted to emulate Him. These choices were not popular, and some were quite challenging to implement. However, I have never looked back or regretted any of my decisions.

I was unexpectedly drawn into the deliverance ministry without knowing anything about it. I was born again in November of 1974 and had my first vision on Easter Sunday in 1975. That's a story for another day. When visions began to appear, I wasn't expecting them. They typically came after I asked God a question. I truly believe we don't do that enough. He loves having conversations with his children and takes delight in teaching us new things.

It's perfectly acceptable to express to God that you don't understand or lack knowledge about certain matters. The Word of God teaches us that if we seek wisdom, He grants it to us freely.

I was born again about a year and a half when I joined the local Ladies Full Gospel Association. The president of the organization was the wife of a Presbyterian minister named Gladys.

When I say I was "born again," I mean that I completely committed to leaving my former life behind and following Jesus with all my heart. I did this, understanding that it would cost me something but knowing the reward would be worth any price. This was a life-altering experience that would change the direction of my life permanently. I hope that describes the kind of commitment every reader of the book has made as well.

One night, Gladys called. My late husband, Joe, picked up the phone. She said, "I'm at a home near you and doing deliverance. I really need some help with prayer. Can you come and pray with me?"

We both agreed. "No problem; we knew how to pray and agreed to do that." When we arrived, we were caught off guard by our surroundings. We could barely navigate this home. Gladys' husband was sitting in the corner, watching and offering no support except for his physical presence. He had an attitude that what Gladys was doing was simply foolishness.

This house was filled with clutter. Boxes were stacked from the floor to the ceiling, leaving only a narrow pathway to walk through. Joe and I zigzagged, carefully maneuvering through the living room and into the kitchen. This is where Gladys had Sherry, the homeowner, seated in a kitchen chair. Gladys was busy commanding demons to leave in the name of Jesus. Joe and I had never witnessed this before, so it was all new to us. We knew from the scriptures that Jesus had commanded demons to leave people, but we'd never seen it happen in a modern-day context.

Gladys paused momentarily and said to us, "Come with me so you can understand what we're dealing with." She was quite exasperated as she explained that she had come to help Sherry clean up after a fire. However, Sherry refused to part with anything in the house, regardless of how damaged or soaked it was with water from putting out the fire. Gladys was baffled by this behavior. She had cast out demons before but had never encountered anything quite like this. It wasn't just Sherry being stubborn; she had a spiritual attachment to seemingly worthless items in her home.

The four of us made our way down a narrow staircase to the basement, where the fire had caused the most damage. There, we found charred magazines and craft supplies piled in heaps across the floor. The pages of the magazines had turned to mush from the water and flames, ultimately becoming a heap of ashes.

The firefighters had sprayed large amounts of water into the basement windows, soaking everything. Smoke covered all the walls and the ceiling. We could barely breathe due to the lingering smell. Everything in the room was drenched. Just touching the magazines made them disintegrate in our hands.

When Gladys arrived earlier and started tossing wet items into the trash, Sherry went "nuts." She cried, "No! No! You can't throw that away." To us, it seemed completely unsalvageable. However, to Sherry, it was like she was losing her best friend.

We watched in amazement as she mourned over the destroyed, useless, burnt rubble. She lovingly picked up an armful of wet, charred treasures. Embracing them closely, she soiled her clothes as she brought them near her heart. She clung to them as if she were in love. It felt as though her very worth was tied up in the debris.

She said again, "No, I can't. I can't throw these things away." With great emphasis, she continued, "I need them! Someday, I'm going to make something out of these." She pointed to what had once been the cover of a magazine showcasing craft items. To the rest of us, the images were unrecognizable. They were merely water-soaked remnants of useless, burned pages.

Sherry had quilting magazines, fabric, needles, and supplies for her quilting projects. She possessed books on floral arrangements and silk flowers for designing and arranging. She owned stained glass magazines and supplies, and the list went on. There was woodworking, carving, knitting, and crocheting supplies and instructions. You name it, Sherry had a magazine and the necessary supplies for it. Yet, she had never even begun any of these projects.

She had established a pattern in her life that repeated endlessly. She would buy a new magazine, feel inspired, and then search for every item she needed for a project at the craft store. Once home with her treasures, the inspiration would fade away. Sherry didn't have a complete craft project for all her efforts. The next day, she would find herself following the same routine with a different magazine and a new inspiration. She kept purchasing more and more supplies nearly every day.

Now, her many treasures lay in the basement, soaked, wet, and smoky from the fire. They were coated in black soot and ashes. Still, Sherry picked them up from the floor and held them close with affection. It was clear that she was obsessed!

Since we weren't showing enough interest in the burnt crafts, Sherry enthusiastically led us to the living room, where she opened one of the hundreds of stacked boxes. She pulled out yet another magazine and proudly displayed all the supplies for her next imagined craft project. That's when we discovered what filled the boxes that stood from the floor to the ceiling in the living room. There were thousands of dollars' worth of craft projects and supplies, and they were everywhere in the house!

Sherry was married to a dentist, but they were now separated. She had moved into her own apartment, and before long, it became cluttered with all sorts of things.

It became clearer to Joe and me what Gladys was dealing with. She took us back to the kitchen and prayed with Sherry once more. Gladys continued to bind and cast out demons while her husband watched silently, curious about what might happen next.

Joe and I had no experience in deliverance. We were merely there for prayer support. As we began to pray in the spirit, I started seeing things I couldn't comprehend. So, I spoke up. I had seen visions before, but never about anyone else. I also didn't realize that I was hearing and seeing demons.

As Gladys prayed, I interrupted her, saying, "I see an iron vice clamped around her midsection, tightening more and more." It took much courage for me to speak up because this was all new to me.

I didn't understand what I was seeing or what it meant. So, I just spoke up and said something. Sometimes, when we witness spiritual things, they appear in a flash, like when we see angels.

In the book of Ezekiel, he saw angels like lightning; they flashed. When we see in the Spirit, we don't always get to see all the details. It's the same with a "word of knowledge" or the "Spirit of Discernment." It feels like you know a secret that no one else knows. Often, it's a matter of insight or understanding.

Don't ignore those flashes. Don't let them catch you off guard. Pay attention! Many times, you may not fully understand what you're seeing. It takes boldness to speak it out and take authority over it. It's okay to be wrong. Engaging in the supernatural requires practice. You'll be surprised at how often you get it right.

> *But strong meat belongeth to them that are of full age, even those who by reason of use have their senses exercised to discern both good and evil. Heb. 5:14*

If you're seeing things, there's a reason. I had no idea how a "Word of Knowledge" worked or why I was having these visions. As soon as I mentioned seeing a vice, Sherry responded, saying, "Oh my God, I have so much pain in my abdomen, but no one could tell me what was causing it."

Secret: Unseen Spirits can apply physical force in this realm.

That's when Gladys told Joe, "Joe, you come over here and cast this thing out." Well, Joe had no idea what to do. As he stood bewildered before Sherry, I heard a word in my head: "Restraint." Restraint? What in the world did that mean? I didn't know, and neither did Joe or Gladys, but it was all we had, so Joe took authority and cast out a spirit of "Restraint." It doesn't seem to make sense even today.

We continued to pray and agree for her deliverance. I could see in her countenance that something was happening. Sherry wasn't showing any emotion.

Joe commanded the spirit of restraint to leave in the name of Jesus. Then, Sherry looked up, her eyes clear, and said, "It's gone." I thought, "It's gone? Just like that? It's gone?" Amazed, she spoke about how the pain around her waist was no longer there. It had been constant, but now it no longer tormented her. She concluded that the demon must be gone if the pain had vanished.

Gladys stepped up and said, "How do you feel?" Sherry proclaimed, "It is gone." None of us were sure we understood what had just happened, so we put it to the test by returning to the basement. Gladys told Sherry, "So, let's start cleaning up this mess."

We wanted to see if Sherry had truly been set free or if she was just pretending. Joe and I certainly weren't experienced enough to know the difference. To our amazement, Sherry bent over, picked up a large armful of burnt magazines, and threw them into the big trash can provided for the cleanup.

I can recall Gladys looking over at Joe and me with an expression that said, "That beats all I've ever seen!" We all began working together to clear the area. We tossed out anything that was wet or scorched. Sherry didn't even want to know what we were discarding. She didn't care. She had been completely set free.

I found it utterly astonishing! An unseen force had taken complete control of this woman's will. Yet, once this hidden influence was exposed and ordered to leave, Sherry was freed from its grasp.

This was my very first deliverance experience, and it made a believer out of me. I went from witnessing a person paralyzed by a demon to seeing her exercise complete freedom in a matter of an hour.

What an incredible God we serve!

Secret: You don't have to understand what you're seeing in the Spirit to exercise authority over it!

I needed to understand what I had just witnessed. I went home and looked up the word "restraint." This is what I found in the dictionary;

a restraining action or influence: Sometimes **restraint** is a means of or device for restraining, as a *harness for the body*.

That is exactly what I saw in the spirit: a harness for the body! The act of restraining means holding back, controlling, or checking.

This described what was happening. Sherry had all these great intentions, but she had been held back from pursuing them. She couldn't bring herself to do what she passionately wanted to do.

Restraint is the state of or fact of being restrained; It is **deprivation of liberty**; It is confinement.

There was a demonic spiritual influence exerted against Sherry to keep her captive. The device I saw around her waist resembled a body harness, just as the definition described. I didn't understand what I was seeing or hearing, but the Spirit of God did.

It was a form of restraint, a controlling force, a deprivation of liberty. The Bible says that where the spirit of the Lord is, there is liberty. However, Sherry had no liberty; she had been restrained and held back from pursuing her desires. Her great creativity had been stifled. She intended to create something beautiful with all the supplies she had purchased, but she couldn't even get started, not even once. She was controlled and restricted by a suffocating demonic force.

This experience sparked a deliverance ministry that grew so quickly that Joe and I felt we had little time for ourselves. Most of the time, we felt like doctors on call.

The happy ending here was that Sherry was filled with the Spirit and reunited with her husband. This marked my first face-to-face battle with the devil. It was just an introduction.

Learning About* "Angelic Assistance in Spiritual Warfare:"

Secret: The Devil goes to Church.

I fully intend to support everything I'm sharing with you by the written Word of God. We're just getting started.

My first experience with Angelic Warfare occurred in the sanctuary of a Baptist church. If you've read my first book, "Letting Them Go, Trusting God to Catch Them," you might remember this incident.

Even though Joe and I were spirit-filled, we still attended the Baptist Church. In the sanctuary, low-hanging lights dangled from long chains strategically placed from a high vaulted ceiling. At the front of the church was a baptistry, while a vast stained-glass window was situated high up in the back of the vaulted roof. Hopefully, you can picture this in your mind's eye.

My two children accompanied us as we entered the sanctuary that Sunday morning. We positioned them between Joe and me in the pew. Our kids were 5 and 9 years old, both of whom had already been saved and baptized. When the music started, it reminded me of merry-go-round tunes—cheerful and lighthearted.

Suddenly, both children started talking and pointing at the ceiling, their voices brimming with unmistakable excitement.

Joe tried to quiet them, but it was in vain. My son, Jeff, said," Dad, we see angels." We didn't know what to make of it. We only knew they were attracting a lot of attention from everyone around us.

Because the service was about to begin, we chose to separate them. We wondered what they had seen to ignite such excitement. Whatever it was, they were both witnessing something that we weren't. After the service, we decided to question them individually to find out if they had seen the same thing.

Later, both children shared the exact same story.

They witnessed this: As we entered the sanctuary and the music began, they saw angels circling above us. Each light hanging from the ceiling had an angel dancing around it, gliding as if in worship. They kept rhythm with the music while circling the light. There were eight lights, each with an angel dressed in long, flowing white garments.

As they watched these angels, a powerful black chariot drawn by black horses suddenly appeared. A fierce black figure was at the reins, which resembled one of the evil characters from "Star Wars." However, this was long before that movie was released.

The chariot stormed out of the baptistry, of all places. The horses galloped fast and furious, full of power as if they had an evil purpose. What happened next was astounding. The children witnessed "Angelic Spiritual Warfare" right there in the rafters of the church.

This malevolent entity came crashing through the rafters of the sanctuary. In response to his presence, the angels worshiping around the lights formed a unified band. They positioned themselves behind the black chariot and propelled it right out the back of the church through that enormous stained-glass window. Wow! I wish I had spiritual eyes to witness this myself.

Evil emerged from the baptistry, thundered through the church, and was ultimately forced out the back. It was vanquished by a host of worshipping angels dressed in white.

Secret: The Worshipping Angels are also Warring Angels.

What a bizarre sight for a couple of kids! They had never encountered anything that would inspire them to invent a story like this, let alone come up with one spontaneously. These weren't even warring angels; they were worshippers. The worshipping angels became warring angels when the need arose. How magnificent is that?

My son was old enough to write down what he observed. He even drew pictures of it. I've maintained a spiritual journal since I was saved and taught the children its importance. So, that day, Jeff included drawings in his journal. That really gave us a clearer understanding of what they had experienced.

Let's consider the implications of this. The setting was a Baptist church on a Sunday morning, where people had gathered to worship God. However, only my children could see this "Angelic Warfare" occurring right in the rafters of the church. If warfare takes place in the church, where else do you think it might happen? In the halls of Congress? At your job? In your living room? Where else?

This spectacular event changed my understanding of church and warfare from that point forward. When we gather to worship, I find myself asking God what kind of attack might be occurring that none of us are aware of. Are demons sent to keep people distracted? To implant thoughts?

Thoughts like, "What are we doing after church? I wonder where so-and-so is today?" Whatever!

I now rarely attend a religious service without starting to bind what I cannot see and asking God to send angels loyal to His throne. At the beginning of a worship service, I often ask the Lord, "What's in the rafters, Father? What should I be aware of and fight for right now?"

Most believers who enter the sanctuary weekly are busy socializing with one another. There's little reverence or understanding of the spiritual realm. They are not even slightly concerned about what might be happening around them that they cannot see. They are entirely focused on what they can see in the world surrounding them.

An unseen realm exists that is just as active, if not more so, than the one we can see.

Secret: Demons are assigned to congregations.

Just ask those who have left witchcraft! A quick search on YouTube will yield many testimonies from former cult members.

This initial encounter with warring angels made me aware of the demonic presence assigned to churches. Seeing in the spirit requires breaking down the barriers between us and our Savior. The things hindering our complete surrender to Him include wounds, hurt, resentments, anger, and unforgiveness. It's a process of healing our broken hearts.

That's what Jesus/Yeshua came to do. He said He came to heal the brokenhearted and to set the captives free. If you feel held captive in any way, Yeshua came to liberate you, and His angels are here to assist in that process. The more we die to self, the more real He and His angels become to us.

> *The Spirit of the Lord is upon me, because he hath anointed me to preach the gospel to the poor; he hath sent me to **heal the brokenhearted**, to preach **deliverance to the captives**, and*

recovering of sight to the blind, to set at liberty them that are bruised, Luke 4:18

Chapter Two

What IS Spiritual Warfare?

Before proceeding, it's important to define "Spiritual warfare."

In Chapter One, we learned that an invisible Angelic Army is ready to assist you in every area of your life. These angels are loyal to God's Throne. They are like our big brothers or older siblings. Sometimes, we can see them, but most of the time, we can't. They remain unseen and invisible.

We have evidence of these armies throughout human history. We are specifically examining the angels mentioned in the scriptures who are recorded as assisting in some capacity of spiritual warfare. Some of these angelic rescues are more evident to the reader than others. Angels have numerous responsibilities, such as being messengers, comforters, judges, counselors, and more.

My intention isn't to provide an exhaustive study of angels but to encourage you to notice what you may have overlooked in reading the Scriptures. It's easy to get caught up in the storyline and miss some of the finer details that make it a truly remarkable event. The angels we focus on here assist both in national and personal battles. What appears to be a personal battle for some turns out to affect the entire nation of Israel and history in general!

God has a purpose and destiny for each of us. His angels work alongside us to help bring that destiny to fruition in our lives. We are about to embrace God's warring angels' powerful and amazing presence. They assist us daily in the spiritual battles we all face. The challenge is that we often fail to recognize the source of those struggles. What's truly behind them? Could an unseen force be the root of our problems?

Not everyone understands what is meant by the term "Spiritual Warfare." Many of you may be familiar with the "Armor of God," explained by the Apostle Paul in Ephesians 6. In that chapter, Paul teaches the believers some fundamentally basic principles of spiritual warfare.

While chapter six may be familiar to some, it's crucial that we don't overlook the first five chapters of this epistle. They address our preparation as we learn to fight the good fight of faith. These chapters reveal the character and nature of our incredible God. They aim to instill in us a desire to emulate Him in every area of our lives.

Our Father wants to see Himself in you! This is essential before we can effectively operate in the full armor of God. God requires loyalty and obedience from those who fight alongside Him and His angelic forces. It would be beneficial to review those chapters to grasp the context of the sixth chapter of Ephesians.

The correct translation is not the "Armor of God" but "God's Armor." God Himself designed this battle garment and provided it for His saints. It's meant to protect us as we fight for the Kingdom of Light. He has equipped us to defend His kingdom and to destroy the works of the devil. John states that Jesus came to destroy the works of the devil, and as His true disciples, we do the same. Our mission is His mission!

> *He that committeth sin is of the devil; for the devil sinneth from the beginning. For **this** purpose, the Son of God was manifested, that he might destroy the works of the devil. 1 Jn.3:8*

Since this book focuses on Angelic Assistance in Warfare, I will only briefly touch on God's Armor in this chapter.

> *Finally, my brethren, be strong in the Lord and in the power of His might. Put on the whole armor of God, that ye may be able to stand against the wiles of the devil. Eph. 6:10-11*

For decades, the church has taught that God's Armor is modeled after the uniform of a Roman soldier. I personally disagree with that model. God never intended for His saints, the warriors of God, to see themselves resembling the image of a pagan Roman soldier in any way.

Secret: Our spiritual armor doesn't resemble that of a Roman soldier!

In contrast, the garments of the Levitical Priesthood were specifically designed by God. When He comes to judge the earth, His army of Saints will return with Him in white linen. These garments belong to the priesthood and to the Bride.

> *Now I saw heaven opened, and behold, a white horse. And He who sat on him was called Faithful and True, and in righteousness He judges and makes* **war.** *His eyes were like a flame of fire, and on His head were many crowns. He had a name written that no one knew except Himself. He was clothed with a robe dipped in blood, and His name is called The Word of God. And the* **armies in heaven,** *clothed in fine linen,* **white** *and clean, followed Him on white horses. Rev. 19:11-14 Amp*

Here's a brief explanation of spiritual warfare for those who have not yet been introduced to its principles or what it entails. When you entered the family of God, you committed to the battle, whether you realized it or not.

Unfortunately, when you walked down the aisle to say your three-minute prayer, you weren't told that you had just put on the uniform of the Kingdom of God. The enemy has now marked you, and he has placed a target on your back.

The scriptures remind us that no soldier goes to war at his own expense or without training. Engaging in spiritual warfare also requires some foundational training, even if, like me, it is through 'on-the-job training."

> *Who serves as a soldier at his own expense? Who plants a vineyard and does not eat its grapes? Who tends a flock and does not drink the milk? 1 Cor. 9:7 NIV*

We are engaged in a cosmic battle between good and evil. The Bible equips believers with strategic tools for spiritual warfare. You are not defenseless; the angels provide you with constant protection. You likely weren't informed of that either.

You and I are called to defend against spiritual deception and the lies of the devil. One of the first things Jesus warns us about in Matt. 24 concerning the End Times is to "not be deceived." Deception is pervasive, and we must stay vigilant, keeping our senses sharp to distinguish good from evil.

> *"But strong meat belongeth to them that are of full age, even those who by reason of use have their senses exercised to **discern both good and evil.**" Heb. 5:14*

Secret: Practice makes perfect!

It is possible not to be deceived. However, we cannot remain strong in the Lord and be empowered by Him without a continuous, intimate connection with Him and with other believers. We're not an army of one; we're a body with many members, and we're stronger together. We need each other and daily intimacy with Yeshua.

Let's begin with some basic understandings:

The scriptures provide evidence for three heavens, and there may be more. It seems there is a first heaven, a second heaven, and a third heaven.

Paul tells us that a man was caught up to the third heaven.

> *I know a man in Christ who fourteen years ago was caught up to the third heaven. 2 Cor. 12:2*

Humankind (you and I) inhabit the first heaven. It follows that if there is a third heaven, there must also be a first and second heaven. The second heaven is where Satan rules his kingdom, which is why he is known as the "Prince of the Power of the Air." The third heaven is God's domain. Understanding this will deepen your insight into what this battle entails.

> *For we do not wrestle against flesh and blood, but against principalities, against powers, against the rulers of the darkness of this age, against spiritual hosts of wickedness in the heavenly places. Eph. 6:12*

Paul informs us that there are three heavens. The first is the one we observe. The physical realm above the earth is where birds fly and clouds drift. The third heaven is the dwelling of God's throne.

We see this example in the following scripture: the wicked spiritual forces are in heavenly places.

> *And there was war in heaven, Michael and his angels waging war with the dragon. The dragon and his angels waged war, and they were not strong enough, and there was no longer a place found for them in heaven. Rev. 12:7-8*

A time will come when Satan no longer rules over the second heaven domain. He will be cast down and will spend his remaining years on Earth.

> *And the great dragon was thrown down, the serpent of old who is called the devil and Satan, who deceives the whole world; he was thrown down to the earth, and his angels were thrown down with him. Rev. 12:9*

As we develop a deeper understanding that we are not alone, we realize that we always have an army of angels by our side. Some fundamental truths will help you grasp who we are fighting, how we do it, and why.

When Satan rebelled against God, he took one-third of the angels with him. These are the forces of darkness that God, His angels, and His family (believers in Jesus/Yeshua) battle against in the earthly realm. Satan and his fallen angels are responsible for all the death, hatred, jealousy, and wickedness on earth. He is the enemy of God and, therefore, the enemy of every born-again Christian. Whether you realize it or not, you are in a battle and have an enemy. Fallen angels come in various shapes and sizes, each with different assignments to kill, steal, or destroy. We believe the following scripture speaks of the rebellion in heaven.

> *"And his tail swept away a third of the stars of heaven and threw them to the earth...." Rev. 12:4*

In the scriptures, stars symbolize angels. If Satan deceived and took a third of the angels with him when he fell, that means two-thirds of the angels remain loyal to the Throne of God. There are more with us than against us. The faithful angels are here to minister to us, the heirs of salvation.

> *Are they not all ministering spirits, sent forth to minister for them who shall be heirs of salvation? Heb. 1:14*

Secret: There is a hidden force behind your daily struggles!

There is a continuous struggle between good and evil that believers experience every day. We often overlook the power or motive behind the challenges we regularly face in our lives and those of our families.

> *Put on the whole armor of God, that ye may be able to stand against the wiles of the devil. Eph.6:11 KJV*

The Amplified Bible refers to God's armor as His precepts. It describes the wiles of the devil as his schemes and strategies for deceiving us.

You are not defenseless. You are hidden with Christ in God. We are meant to understand God's precepts. We have been provided with every weapon necessary to engage in battle and do so effectively.

Definition: **Precepts**:

1. a rule *or principle prescribing a particular course of action* or **conduct**.

2. A direction or **order** issued by an authority, a command or **process**,

3. A commandment or direction given as a **rule of action**: teaching; instruction; especially an injunction as to moral conduct, a **rule of conduct**.

The Word tells us that Satan is a deceiver; he has been a liar from the very beginning. His goal is to trick you. We're up against schemes, strategies, and deceptions devised by the devil himself. If he deceived a third of the angels, would it be possible for you to be deceived as well? This is why we must remain close to Yeshua/Jesus.

So, we're asking God to alert us to the enemy's schemes. We ask, "What are his strategies, God? Open our eyes wide to see what is coming." The Devil is exceptionally deceitful, and he will attempt to deceive us at every opportunity.

You are not fully prepared for war if you don't know the Word of God, His handbook for the battle. The devil will catch you off guard. If you try to fight on your own terms, you won't succeed. We must play by God's rules. To do that, you must know the rulebook. The devil knows who understands the rules and who doesn't. He aims to catch you unaware. He is a bully. The younger you are and the quicker he can trap you, the more satisfied he becomes.

Satan feeds on the force of iniquity. Sin is his food. The more prevalent sin is in society, the more power he gains.

Secret: Satan's food is the force of iniquity!

We must be able to hear well enough to receive orders when the Holy Spirit speaks. We get these orders through our inner voice, the Holy Spirit within, or even from angels. God has a process, a plan, and a timetable that only He can reveal to us. When I say you are required to know the Word, you must understand that Yeshua is the Word. He is both the written Word and the spoken Word. Your voice gives His written Word power when you speak it and release it into the world. If we learn to hear Jesus speak, we will realize that every answer to every question lies within you, because the spirit of Jesus himself lives inside of you! Ponder that for a minute!

That's how wielding the sword of the Spirit works. You speak it, and it is released into the earth through vibrations and frequencies. The Word of God never returns to Him void or empty; it accomplishes what He sent it forth to achieve. When you speak it, it goes forth, works, and produces God's desired outcome.

> *So shall my word be that goeth forth out of my mouth: it shall not return unto me void, but it shall accomplish that which I please, and it shall prosper in the thing whereto I sent it. Is. 55:11*

None of us truly know all of the Word. Some are more learned than others. If you spend time in God's presence, He will provide for whatever you lack. He's searching for willing vessels. I hope that you are one of them. He is looking for you.

How often do you buy something new and try to use it without reading the manual? How's that working out for you? God has given us a manual for living on this planet: The Bible. He created this earth and shows us how to live in harmony within the environment He made for us. If we had consulted the manual first, we wouldn't have made so many mistakes or had so many messes to clean up later. Instead, we prefer to do things our own way, relying on our own wisdom rather than turning to the guidance and principles of God.

Secret: Things go better when you read the instructions!

You and I are people of "The Covenant." We have stepped across the threshold of God's house and are now adopted into His family. When we enter through His threshold, God Himself takes responsibility for our well-being. Our duty is to follow the rules of His house. We are called to be members of God's family, and in His household, there are rules and regulations that He expects us to follow. We recognize that by grace, we are saved through the blood of Jesus, and by that alone! We're not trying to earn favor with God. We simply wish to please our King as we live in His Kingdom.

When the blood of Jesus cleanses our unclean hearts, we desire to do the will of the Father. We want to please Him with all our hearts because we love Him. Our obedience is not motivated by the desire to earn anything; rather, it stems from our love for God.

As obedient brides, we reflect His selfless love. We should be so infatuated with Him that we passionately propose to do His will. As we behold Him, we become like Him. His character is ingrained in each of us as His warring saints. We are His preparing bride.

Continue to behold Him. Keep focusing on His Word, observing His character daily, and you will become like Him.

> *Beloved, now are we the sons of God, and it doth not yet appear what we shall be: but we know that, when he shall appear, we shall be like him; for we shall see him as he is. And every man that hath this hope in him purifieth himself, even as he is pure. 1 Jn. 3:2-3*

He will return in His glorified body, and we, too, will shed this earthly flesh, putting on glorified bodies. He will know us, and we will know Him. He is building His character in us each day. We will not function well in God's armor unless we begin to display His character.

Let's look at Eph 6:10 again in the Amplified version:

> *..........be strong in the Lord [draw your strength from Him and be empowered through your union with Him] and in the power of His (boundless) might. Eph. 6:10*

Our strength comes from the Lord as we remain in His presence. It takes time to learn how to still ourselves, block out the world, and simply be with Him. When we do, He tells us things.

> *Call unto me, and I will answer thee, and shew thee great and mighty things, which thou knowest not. Jer. 33:3*

Stay committed to it if you are just getting to know God more intimately. Dedicate time to this pursuit every day. Soon, you will be better equipped to fight the good fight of faith than many others. You will have caught up to and surpassed those who have never invested time in knowing Him more deeply. It's never too late. Ask God to place you on an accelerated path. It simply takes your desire, and the Holy Spirit will work with you to know Jesus/Yeshua more completely. When you do that, you will begin to develop spiritual eyes to see and ears to hear.

As believers, we carry His presence with us when we enter any room. You start to radiate a glow. Nothing truly matters except that you have been in His presence and are taking it wherever you go. It's the glow of God that makes a person beautiful. It's not about your outward appearance; it's about who you are inside. Even if you are physically challenged, God's light will draw others to you. They will desire to be close to you. That should be our goal: to embody the presence of God.

You cannot be strong in the Lord and the Power of His might without a continual intimate relationship with Him and other believers. It takes all of us to make up His body. His presence within us is the Hope of Glory, but you alone do not encompass the entirety of who the Messiah is. This is an exchange. We learn who Christ is by understanding how He relates to us and watching how He is impacting others' lives. God desires that all believers become one in Him. We need each other. Again, we are not an army of one; we are a body with many members and stronger together.

Secret: *Gathering with others to pray or do warfare multiplies your power exponentially!*

> *For where two or three are gathered together in my name, there am I in the midst of them. Matt 18:20*

We have seen this as we come together to pray and engage in spiritual warfare. The gathering of sincere, dedicated believers appears to evoke the presence of angels. We know, without a doubt, that Jesus/Yeshua is among us because the Word says so.

It's beneficial to examine your motives periodically. Ask yourself, "Am I doing things for myself or for recognition?" If so, you're engaging in selfishness and self-love rather than selflessness.

The Ten Commandments teach us not to take what belongs to others. They encourage us to be selfless. Yeshua/Jesus exemplifies selfless love; we become like Him when we behold Him. If we do this, we won't need commandments to direct our behavior. Instead, we'll show the character of God to everyone around us. We are called to love others more than we love ourselves.

> *"For you died to this life, and your real life is hidden with Christ in God. Col. 3:3*

So, what does that look like? This earth is NOT our home. We need to establish that in our minds. We must recognize that we are sojourners. This is a temporary place; when we leave here, we merely change our addresses. We don't cease to exist; we are simply changing addresses.

We are just like Abraham in Canaan. He sojourned for years in that land, believing it would be given to him one day. Canaan is what became Israel. From the time God made the promise to him until they entered the land as a nation, four hundred years passed. We, too, are on a journey, and what we long to see may not be realized in our lifetime. Even so, what we do on this earth matters. It matters for future generations. Our actions and words leave their mark on this earth even after we're gone.

My late brother-in-law, who served in the military, described how they could extract past conversations from the mountains of Hawaii. He was part of a team that retrieved radio transmissions related to the enemy's attack on Pearl Harbor. This provided the military with Detailed information about what occurred that day during the attacks. The radio waves captured in the mountains had been stored there indefinitely. This confirmed for me what the scriptures have stated about our words.

> *But I say unto you, That every idle word that men shall speak, they shall give account thereof in the day of judgment. Matt. 12:36*

Secret: You will be held accountable for every word spoken!

Every word we speak is recorded. We will be held accountable for those words. They are recorded somewhere on this earth. If we tell a lie or even a partial truth, there's a record of that lie. If we don't accurately represent who God is to the world, we will be held accountable for that misrepresentation.

This is the key: dying to this life doesn't occur just once; it happens daily, even hourly, and sometimes minute by minute. We must not be concerned about what others think or say about us when we choose to live and act according to the Word of God.

Secret: If the devil can't get to you, he will find someone else who can.

The devil's weapons are his **words**. He will distract you with **words** that can wound you. He will use **words** to send fiery darts your way. He will target someone you love who can affect you if he cannot get to you personally. He will do his utmost to inflict pain with **words.**

As we continue in Eph. 6

> *Your hand-to-hand combat is not with human beings, but with the highest principalities and authorities operating in rebellion under the heavenly realms. For they are a powerful class of*

demon-gods and evil spirits that hold this dark world in bondage. Eph. 6:12 TPT

Often, the enemy seems to take on a physical form as another person, but what is motivating that person and influencing the words they say?

The rule of thumb is that God convicts us of sin; however, if it is condemnation, that feeling comes from the devil, not from God. God does not condemn. He never makes you feel like a failure or that you will never be good enough.

Recently, I asked a young person about the revivals occurring on his college campus, and he responded, "I don't know anything about that. I've been feeling depressed and have just stayed in my dorm room alone."

Who wins in this situation? Not God. That's when we need to take authority over the spirit of depression and say, "No, no depression, you are not welcome here in Jesus' name. Get out of my life." What does the devil gain if he can get a young Christian man to isolate himself in his room? He has come to kill, steal, and destroy. He is just getting started. We MUST fight back.

Ephesians 6:12 discusses the worldly forces of the present darkness. Today, we can see the global forces at play more clearly than ever. We experienced a worldwide pandemic driven by forces manipulating every aspect of life on the planet that they could. Praise God, they could not control everything but took advantage wherever they found an open door. They did it with **words**.

We are battling global forces—not just local entities trying to control our cities, but world powers acting as if they are gods. These are spiritual forces operating from the heavens. These are world forces; demons influence and use powerful humans. Some of them believe that they themselves are gods. They are not! There is only one true God, Yahweh!

Spiritual Forces of Wickedness in the Heavenlies:

These originate from supernatural realms. There is a force behind the darkness we observe. It underlies all the wickedness occurring. These forces influence much of what we are informed about, particularly if it comes from the mainstream media. Even when the adversary appears in flesh and blood, ask yourself, what's the force behind that individual? Who is manipulating that person? Who's pulling the puppet strings? They can use vicious, accusatory language that makes you feel as though they are crushing your very essence. But where do their words originate? Who is behind them? Who is the one who comes to kill, steal, and destroy? That's right. Recognize that this person is being driven by the enemy.

Those kinds of words are meant to curse you. Reverse the curse! When hateful words are thrown at you, send them back to the sender. Not by returning words of hate but by declaring that they hold no power over you in the name of Jesus! The book of Proverbs tells us that the causeless curse shall not come. If you have not earned a curse, then send it back to where it originated. If you recognize that you have done something to bring it on, then repent. God is forgiving, and He will turn things around for you when you repent. Use the authority of His name and His blood! Reverse that curse!

Secret: You can reverse the curse!

> *Therefore, put on the complete armor of God, so that you will be able to [successfully] resist and stand your ground in the evil day [of danger], and having done everything [that the crisis demands], to stand firm [in your place, fully prepared, immovable, victorious]. Eph. 6:13 Amp.*

Wear the full armor of God, not just part of it. Our goal is to resist successfully. We must not yield. We must not comply. We should never lie down and cower. We're meant to resist the Devil because when we do, he will flee from us in terror.

> *"Submit yourselves therefore to God. Resist the devil, and he will flee from you." James 4:7*

The first line of defense remains consistent: submit yourself to God. When you do this, Satan flees. Worship is a powerful way to submit to God, as it sends the devil running every time.

In our lives, we encounter crises that require immediate action. I'm quite sure we will face even more in the future. Our best initial response is to say to God, "What? What do You want? What are You trying to achieve in me? Is this about me? Is this about someone else? Is it about the earth? How do you want me to respond? What is YOUR battle plan? I want to align with what You have in mind."

When we follow the instructions, we are able to stand firm. Crises will happen. We may not always be physically and emotionally prepared for them, but in spirit, we can be fully ready in an instant. Regardless of the nature of the crisis—whether it's an environmental disaster, an earthquake, a storm, or an accident—what will your first response be? In any situation, we need supernatural wisdom. Begin praying now that you will act wisely in every circumstance and avoid panic. The enemy relies on your panic; he is the author of terror, promoting fear at every turn. The Bible says that fear brings torment.

God has not given us the spirit of fear:

> *For God hath not given us the spirit of fear; but of power, and of love, and of a sound mind. 2 Tim. 1:7*

> *There is no fear in love; but perfect love casteth out fear: because fear hath torment. He that feareth is not made perfect in love. 1 Jn. 4:18*

He has given us power, love, and soundness of mind. We need not panic. It is the tormentor who seeks to instill fear in you. The closer we draw to Jesus, the less fear we will experience.

To resist is to oppose. We are the opposing team. We are the winning team. We've read the end of the book! An evil day of danger is upon us. It's here. Continue to pray for angelic protection. Guard your DNA daily; there is a persistent plan to attack our Godly makeup. Pray for your surroundings. Pray against devastating destruction, storms, and fires, for protection against chemical spills, and against any threats to your ability to breathe. These are just a few ways that the enemy is waging war against humanity.

When a crisis strikes, we must not falter but do everything that the situation demands. We are warriors! We are the remnant, and we must stand firm, unyielding, and triumphant. We can't retreat to our rooms, close the door, and accept being depressed. We don't have that luxury.

Every time you do that, the enemy gains ground in your life. Then you must fight harder to reclaim that mountain or hill again.

This reminds me of what occurred in the Vietnam War. Our soldiers fought to the death to capture a hill. Then, just a few days later, they received orders to move on, abandoning the hill they had just conquered. This allowed the enemy to reclaim that hill, rendering their struggle and loss of life futile. Don't let the devil do that in your life. Don't allow the enemy to take any part of your life. Don't give him an inch; he won't give one to you. He never plays fairly. When you are kind, he is not. He doesn't negotiate. He has one agenda: to kill anyone who bears the name of Jesus/Yeshua. We are the remnant; we must be steadfast and victorious.

> *Therefore, my beloved brothers and sisters, be steadfast, immovable, always excelling in the work of the Lord [always doing your best and doing more than is needed], being continually aware that your labor [even to the point of exhaustion] in the Lord is not futile nor wasted [it is never without purpose]. 1 Co. 15:58 Amp.*

Immovable means that you are incapable of movement. You will not move off your confession of faith.

> *So stand firm and hold your ground, HAVING TIGHTENED THE WIDE BAND OF TRUTH (personal integrity, moral courage) AROUND YOUR WAIST and HAVING PUT ON THE BREASTPLATE OF RIGHTEOUSNESS (an upright heart), (this comes from Is. 11:5 speaking of Yeshua) We are to be like him. Eph. 6:14 Amp.*

Stand your ground. The belt of Truth is a broadband. We must be truth-tellers. Even little white lies are significant. You can't stretch the truth. You can't merely say things to please others. Every word you utter is noted.

If you must lie to prevent someone from losing their life, we see in the Word that sometimes this is permitted.

The reality is that those "little white lies" you tell are often to avoid discomfort. Speaking the truth reflects your integrity. Can God trust what you say?

To engage in battle effectively, we must be people of truth. We want God to trust our words. We cannot bless and curse with the same mouth and expect our words to be powerful in battle. Watching what we say is not bondage; it's discipline. We train our mouths to align with the truth of God's WORD. It's never too late to learn God's ways and His Words. We ask, what is truth?

Many people are asking this today. They don't know who they can trust. Well, the answer is:

> *Sanctify them through thy truth: thy word is truth. Jn. 17:17*

People are skeptical these days. They don't trust the government or their doctors, and certainly, they don't trust the media. The only thing we can trust is God.

> *The sum of your word is truth, and every one of your righteous rules endures forever. Ps. 119:160*

It's not just a part of God's Word that is truth. It cannot be taken out of context to prove a point. It is the complete sum of His Word that represents truth. From Genesis to Revelation is truth. His righteous rules endure forever. Never forget that. He is the same yesterday, today, and forever. There is no shadow of turning in Him. He is altogether righteous and altogether holy.

> *and having strapped on YOUR FEET THE GOSPEL OF PEACE IN PREPARATION [to face the enemy with firm-footed stability and the readiness produced by the **good news**]. Eph. 6:15 Amp.*

> *How beautiful on the mountains are **the feet** of those who bring **good news**, who proclaim peace, who bring good tidings, who proclaim salvation, who say to Zion, "You God reigns." Is. 52:7*

We are the ones who bring the GOOD news! We proclaim the truth to a hurting and dying world. Every day, we speak words of salvation through our actions. What we do and how we behave show God's work in our lives. We declare that our God reigns, and we are not ashamed of the gospel of peace. We shout it from the rooftops. Our God reigns!!!!

> *Above all, lift up the [protective] shield of faith with which you can extinguish all the flaming arrows of the evil one. **Eph. 6:16 Amp.***

With the shield of faith, the arrows shot at you will be extinguished. The arrows are the plans of the enemy against you. It takes faith to extinguish them. Sometimes, it feels like the arrows come in a relentless barrage. They are ALL repelled by your faith. As you get proficient in using your shield, what used to trouble you day and night no longer affects you. You don't take the bait of Satan. You refuse to play his game of torment. Our faith always remains in Yeshua. When we are falsely accused, God will vindicate us.

> *And take THE HELMET OF SALVATION, and the sword of the Spirit, which is the Word of God. Eph. 6:17*

We are asked to do as Yeshua has done. He does what He asks us to do.

> *The Lord looked and was displeased that there was no justice. He saw that there was no one, he was appalled that there was no one to intervene; so **his own arm** achieved salvation for him, and his own righteousness sustained him. He put on righteousness as his **breastplate**, and the **helmet** of salvation on his head; he put on the **garments** of vengeance and wrapped himself in zeal as in a cloak. Is. 59:16-17*

It is amazing to realize that Isiah records the Armor of God. These words didn't originate from Paul. He was preaching from the prophets, as he should be.

And then, with all prayer:

> *With all prayer and petition pray [with specific requests] at all times [on every occasion and in every season] in the Spirit, and with this in view, stay alert with all perseverance and petition [interceding in prayer] for all God's people. Eph. 6:18 Amp.*

So, what is warfare? What does it look like? It's not merely what we do in prayer; how we live makes our words powerful in the battle of words.

One evening, during a group prayer, I witnessed a powerful example of what this scripture conveys. I experienced an open vision of Satan, who appeared fiery red and blazing with flames. He lunged forward in extreme anger, wielding a weapon in his hand, though I couldn't discern what it was. The most obvious feature about him was his mouth. It was open wide as if he were about to devour something or someone. Later, as I prayed, I asked God, "What was the weapon in his hand?" He responded, "Sharon, what did you see?" I replied, "I saw a huge mouth." He said, "That's because THAT IS his weapon. His **mouth** is his weapon!" The mouth was so large and vicious that it didn't matter what was in his hand. His real weapon was his mouth. His words! This is how he deceives the world. Maybe the weapon he held was deception!

Secret: Never forget, that the devil's greatest weapon is his mouth!

> *And the beast was **given a mouth** (the power of speech), uttering great things and arrogant and blasphemous words, and he was given freedom and authority to act and to do as he pleased for forty-two months (three and a half years). Rev. 13:5*

He battles with his words. So do we. We have the power to speak. We are supposed to use it. We have the right and the power to speak. We should be doing that.

Then I asked, "Why was the devil so angry?" God responded, "Because he knows his time is short. People like you and your team are praying and throwing stumbling blocks in his way. He is furious with the Saints of God who pray."

It will be words that deceive the world, convincing them to engage in activities that may cause them to lose out on an eternity with God. Words will persuade them—lies. Satan is the father of lies; he has been a liar from the beginning.

So, what does warfare look like? It is intense prayer, intercession, and spoken words. God's words are conveyed through you and me. We confront the enemy's words with God's words. We issue rebukes and command demons to depart in the name of Jesus.

When Jesus comes, He will destroy Satan with the breath of His mouth. We fight against Satan's words with God's words! If you have a prayer language, allow the Spirit to intercede through you with the words of the Holy Spirit. This is an explosive weapon of warfare. You never have to wonder if you are praying according to your own will instead of God's.

> *"And then shall that Wicked be revealed, whom the Lord shall **consume with the spirit of his mouth**, and shall destroy with the brightness of his coming:" 2 Thes. 2:8*

Now that we have a clearer understanding of what Spiritual Warfare is let's explore a concept that will enhance our understanding of the role of angels in supporting us during our spiritual battles. This will be a fascinating journey. Thank you for joining me on this adventure.

There are more detailed teachings on Spiritual Warfare that can be found at: www.YouTube.com/Sharoncluck.

Chapter 3

Jacob's Angelic Rescue

Secret: Three Angels can appear as 2000 men.

As we embark on this exciting journey together, you'll discover that a couple of the accounts I share with you come from historical writings, and all others are drawn directly from scripture. This first account, titled "Angelic Rescue," details a stunning and miraculous deliverance orchestrated by three warring angels. It stands as one of my absolute favorite victory stories from antiquity. I encourage you to seek out this story and read it in its entirety; it's truly spectacular! Many of you have probably never encountered this story before, as it is found in the book of Jasher. Although Jasher is not a canonized book of the Bible, it is rich with stories that genuinely glorify God.

The Book of Jasher is referenced in the Bible. You'll find it mentioned in Joshua 10:13 and Second Samuel 2:18. Both these passages direct us to further detail that can be found in the Book of Jasher, proving that this book clearly dates to the time of Joshua when the walls of Jericho miraculously fell. That, too, was achieved with the help of angelic assistance. We'll learn more about that in the following chapters.

The Book of Jasher is said to have been rescued during the burning of the temple in 70 AD by a Roman centurion. He sent it to Sephardic Jews in Spain, where it remained until the Jews were expelled from Spain by Ferdinand in 1492. The word "Jasher" means the Book of the Upright or the "Book of the Just Man." It wasn't written by a person named Jasher. Historian Josephus recognized it as one of the books stored in the Temple.

The writings of Jasher correspond with "The Genesis Apocryphon," found among "The Dead Sea Scrolls." *

This book later showed up in Venice in 1813, written in the Hebrew language. It was translated into English in 1840. Although we don't refer to this book as "scripture," it is, however, accepted as an ancient history book. I've found it to enhance my personal studies of the Torah, the first five books of the Bible, greatly.

The Book of Jasher provides deeper insight into the characters of the patriarchs. Many of these details are not apparent in the canonized scriptures. It gives readers a better understanding of the intricate struggles of the patriarchs and their incredible, miraculous victories. Understanding how God rescues through angelic intervention brings even more glory to our Great God and King. This is one of the reasons I felt compelled to begin with this story.

The Bible is one book with limited space. Because of that, it's not possible to include everything happening behind the scenes. It goes without saying that humans normally see only what is visible to their human eyes. There are events happening on our behalf in the spirit realm that we may never know about. You'll witness that in this next story.

That's why inquisitive minds like mine truly appreciate learning more about "the rest of the story." The additional detail brings the Biblical account to life before our eyes. It deepens our understanding of well-known stories.

I'm not suggesting that the Bible isn't sufficient by itself; it certainly is. It summarizes events and what we "need to know." We must remember that many individuals have sacrificed their lives to ensure our access to God's written Word. Nevertheless, we can now explore more of the backstories

*Ant.5:1:17, http://nazarenespace.com/blog/2020/12/21/the-lost-book-of-jasher-and-the-dead-sea-scrolls/

with recent discoveries. These insights help us grasp some of the motives behind the actions in God's Word.

The Dead Sea Scrolls were discovered in 1947, verifying the accuracy of the Bible. Among these ancient scrolls was found the scroll of Jasher. Its content answers many questions that naturally arise as we study the scriptures. The story of Jacob's angelic rescue is filled with details that thrilled me when I first read it. It comes from Jasher 32, starting with verse 26. You'll find the corresponding story beginning in Genesis 27 in your Bible. So, let me set the stage for you.

As a young man, Jacob and his brother Esau had a feud over who should receive the family birthright. When Esau threatened to kill Jacob, their mother, Rebecca, instructed him to escape to his Uncle Laban's house in Syria. She believed he would be safe there from the fury of his brother's wrath. From the outset, Laban began mistreating Jacob. As the years went by, they came to distrust one another greatly. Jacob labored for Laban for over twenty years; even though he was family, he was treated like a servant.

> *yet your father has cheated me by changing my wages ten times. However, God has not allowed him to harm me. Gen. 31:7 NIV*

Jacob endured many tests and hardships during this time. Throughout this season of his life, God worked wonders in his heart. It's a long, complicated story, so I'll jump to just one of the amazing encounters with angels in Jacob's life; there were many.

This chapter begins with Jacob fleeing from Laban. They were parting on bad terms. God spoke to Jacob, instructing him to return home to his Father. Jacob was the heir to the promises made to his grandfather Abraham. He was blessed with the family birthright and was being sent back to the land that God had promised. God assured Jacob that He would accompany him.

When Jacob first arrived at Laban's, he had only his clothes on his back and his staff. Now, he returned as a wealthy man with a family, servants, and numerous flocks. His two wives, Rachel and Leah, and their eleven children traveled with him. He feared that Esau, his brother, would come out to meet him upon learning of his return to the land. This filled him with great distress and concern for his life and his family's safety. He knew that his brother had not lost his passion or desire to take his life.

Laban, who was angry with Jacob, sent messengers ahead to Esau to inform him of Jacob's return. Laban's anger toward Jacob refueled Esau's hatred. He had never relented from his vow to kill his brother.

Jacob knew he would be confronted with a life-and-death situation, not only for himself but also for his entire family. His sole hope was to call upon the God of his ancestors, Abraham and Isaac. That was his only chance of survival.

He decided to send his family and servants ahead of him. Desperate to seek the face of God, he needed to be alone. He had encountered God in this place, "Bethel," once before. He trusted that God would appear to him again amid his distress. Jacob was committed during his time of prayer. He fought all night in the spirit for himself, his family, and the destiny passed down to him from his ancestors. The outcome of his passionate, fervent prayers exceeded Jacob's imagination. The Angel of the Lord, Himself, appeared!

Many believe that this angel was the pre-incarnate Christ. This time of prayer was so intense that Jacob and the angel wrestled. It was so literal that Jacob sustained physical injuries from this encounter. By morning, Jacob had prevailed. During this struggle, Jacob was struck on the hip and would walk with a limp from that day forward. I can't even imagine this kind of spiritual warfare; it's beyond anything I have ever experienced or known of. This was the night that God changed Jacob's name to Israel. He had prevailed with God.

Secret: Remember from Sherry's story that things that happen in the spirit may manifest in the physical.

This blows me away. How does one prevail with God?

Jacob's character has changed drastically due to his many life experiences. Now, he has encountered the "Angel of the Lord" face to face. When God transforms our character, He gives us a new name. We know this because the scriptures tell us that a new name is written down in glory for each of us, and nobody knows it except Yeshua. It is our unique name.

That night, as Jacob wrestled with the angel, he reminded Yahweh that he was obeying His instructions by returning to his family. He had been obedient, and it seemed like it would cost him his life. He expected God to protect him on this journey, but what he saw and heard filled him with doubt and fear.

We refer to living for Jesus as "a walk of faith." We cannot allow ourselves to believe solely what our physical eyes perceive. This has become increasingly apparent in the times we live in. We have no reliable way of knowing whether what we see is truly real. We can't believe our eyes. Therefore, we must rely even more on the Word of God. It's the only thing we can absolutely trust to be true!

Jacob had sent his servants ahead of him, carrying gifts for Esau to appease him. That approach proved effective for Jacob in the past, but Esau wasn't interested; he wanted to kill his brother. Instead, the servants returned with a grim report: "Esau is on his way; he has 400 warriors with him, and he is more determined than ever to kill you."

Sometimes, we must reject what we see or hear. We must resist believing malicious reports from the enemy, no matter who is delivering the news. That's why we ask, "Whose report will you believe?" We should trust the report of the Lord!

What did God say? He told Jacob to return to his father, Isaac. God promised Jacob that his descendants would be like the sands of the sea.

Jacob could battle through this if his faith were strong enough to hold onto God's words. It wasn't what the servants reported that was most important; what God had said mattered most. We all have our battles. You must remember and reflect on what God has spoken to you personally and through His written Word. That will sustain you through every trial.

> *And Jacob tarried there that night, and during the whole night he gave his servants instructions concerning the forces and his children. And the Lord heard the prayer of Jacob on that day, and the Lord then delivered Jacob from the hands of his brother Esau. And the Lord sent three angels of the angels of heaven, and they went before Esau and came to him. Jasher 32:26-27*

This is how God delivered Jacob. He didn't reveal His plan to Jacob or how He would carry it out. God certainly had a plan and was about to execute it without Jacob's awareness. God never ceases working on our behalf. Even when we don't see it, He's working!

Secret: God doesn't need to reveal how He works on YOUR behalf. He simply does it!

The Lord sent three angels from heaven. Only these three angels could appear as 2,000 men. Can you even imagine that?

We've heard stories about the Six-Day War in Israel in 1967. There was no way, in a natural sense, that Israel should have won this war. They were outnumbered and under-equipped militarily. Here is a short paragraph to give you an idea of how God intervened.

"One Israeli infantry recruit, on patrol with one other soldier, reported an encounter with a truck loaded with 18 well-armed Egyptian soldiers. The two Israelis, equipped with inadequate weapons, believed they faced certain death. However, the Arabs, looking panic-stricken, did not fire on them and complied immediately when the Israeli soldier then shouted, "Hands up!" Later, he asked an Egyptian sergeant why they hadn't shot at the Israeli soldiers. The reply: "My arms froze—they became paralyzed. My whole body was paralyzed, and I don't know why." *

To God be the glory! He is the same yesterday, today and forever!

So, how did God save Jacob?

> *And these angels appeared unto Esau and his people as two thousand men, riding upon horses furnished with all sorts of war instruments, and they appeared in the sight of Esau and all his men to be divided into four camps, with four chiefs to them. Jasher 32:29*

There are three angels, appearing as 2,000 men divided into four camps of 500 each. Esau had a total of 400 men accompanying him with the intent to kill Jacob. That's a lot of men to take down one person, along with his servants and family. Now, Esau's forces are outnumbered by each of these angelic camps that he is destined to confront.

It states that the angelic warriors are equipped with various weapons of war. I found this amusing because I have had the privilege of catching a glimpse of Yahweh's armory. The armies of Satan possess nothing compared to the Armies of God and their weaponry.

> *And one camp went on and they found Esau coming with four hundred men toward his brother Jacob, and this camp ran toward Esau and his people and **terrified them**, and Esau fell off the horse in alarm, and all his men separated from him in that place, for they were greatly afraid. Jasher 32: 30*

*https://cbnisrael.org/2022/06/09/fulfilling-gods-promises-the-miracles-of-israels-six-day-war/

https://www.chabad.org/multimedia/timeline_cdo/aid/525324/jewish/June-8-Day-4.htm

A "camp" is roughly the size of a half regiment in our modern army. It's a group of warriors. The angel army charged on horseback, thundering toward Esau and his men, and all of Esau's men fled. The book of Jasher reveals in several places how the loud noises of these Hebrew tribes and angels are utilized in warfare. No wonder their enemies were terrified. The ground shook, and dust flew everywhere. Horses snorted, and warriors shouted. The noise alone would have completely unnerved them. This was clearly a surprise attack. Esau's army certainly wasn't prepared to face this level of resistance.

This book recounts numerous tales of battle skirmishes. It reveals how the screeches of warriors like Judah and Issachar are so alarming that they debilitate entire armies. We don't know what they sounded like, but they were very effective in battle. Perhaps the tribes of Israel learned these terrifying battle cries from the intimidating angels.

> *And the whole of the camp shouted after them when they fled from Esau, and all the warlike men (these are angels) answered, saying, Surely we are the servants of Jacob, who is the servant of God, (They are exalting Jacob in the eyes of his brother Esau, they are saying we are the servants of Jacob, who is the servant of the most high God.) and who then can stand against us? And Esau said unto them, O then, my lord and brother Jacob is your lord, whom I have not seen for these twenty years, and now that I have this day come to see him, do you treat me in this manner? Jasher 32: 31-32*

Suddenly, Esau conveniently referred to Jacob as his Lord.

> *And the angels answered him saying, As the Lord liveth, were not Jacob of whom thou speaketh thy brother, we had not let one remaining from thee and thy people, but only on account of Jacob we will do nothing to them. And this camp passed from Esau and his men and it went away, and Esau and his men had gone from them about a league when the second camp came toward him with*

> *all sorts of weapons, and they also did unto Esau and his men as the first camp (angels) had done to them. And when they had left it to go on, behold the third camp came toward him and they were all terrified, and Esau fell off the horse, and the whole camp cried out, and said, Surely we are the servants of Jacob, who is the servant of God, and who can stand against us? Jasher 32:35*

I find this incredibly entertaining! Now, Esau has faced three armies that oppose him. Each army is larger than his own, and all are on horseback, armed to the teeth.

> *And Esau again answered them saying, O then, Jacob my lord and your lord is my brother, and for twenty years I have not seen his countenance and hearing this day that he was coming, I went this day to meet him, and do you treat me in this manner? And they answered him, and said unto him, As the Lord liveth, were not Jacob thy brother as thou didst say, we had not left a remnant from thee and thy men, but on account of Jacob of whom thou speakest being thy brother, we will not meddle with thee or thy men. Jasher 32:36-37*

Secret: Angels will speak for you!

This is how angels fight for you and me. They are out there advocating for us. They say, "I have come on behalf of my brother or sister." They have gone to war for you. Because you serve God, they are battling for you!

> *And the third camp also passed from them, and he still continued his road with his men toward Jacob, when the fourth camp came toward him, and they also did unto him and his men as the others had done. And when Esau beheld the evil which the four angels had done to him and to his men,* **he became greatly afraid of his brother Jacob,** *and he went to meet him in* **peace.** *Jasher 32:38-39*

The night before, Jacob prayed all night because he was afraid of his brother. Now the tables have turned with "Angelic Assistance in Warfare," and Esau is the one who fears Jacob.

Jacob may not have a physical army like Esau does, but he possesses a band of angels that can never be defeated by Esau's natural men. Hallelujah! The Lord lives!

And remember this: only three angels were sent to fight for Jacob, yet they appeared to be 2,000 warriors. No wonder the Word of God says that one can chase a thousand, and two can put ten thousand to flight. Hallelujah! Bless the Lord forevermore! Can you see why this story thrills my heart?

Esau went to meet Jacob peacefully. His anger has been calmed by the angelic assistance sent to fight for Jacob.

> *And Esau concealed his hatred against Jacob, because he was afraid of his life on account of his brother Jacob, and because he imagined that the four camps that he had lighted upon were Jacob's servants. Jasher 32:40*

Every time I read this account, I shake my head in amazement. Jacob wrestled in prayer all night with the angel. The response was that God sent four camps of troops against Esau. Only God knew what would change Esau's heart and mind. God sent His angels to intimidate the enemy. I love it!

Satan loves to intimidate the children of God. Know that even when you don't see it, God will push him back on your behalf. Our God is a Man of War and cannot be defeated.

> *No weapon that is formed against thee shall prosper; and every tongue that shall rise against thee in judgment thou shalt condemn. This is the heritage of the servants of the LORD, and their righteousness is of me, saith the LORD. Is. 54:17*

I have seen angels manifest in response to our prayers. They often come for protection, reassurance, and comfort, as well as to rescue us. They are present whether you realize it or not. Jacob did not understand why Esau approached in peace. It resulted from his wrestling and spiritual warfare.

You are surrounded by a myriad of angels all the time. They are waiting to assist you. You do not command them. Jacob did not command them, but he prayed, and when he prevailed, God sent the troops.

Jacob had no idea how God would rescue him, but he fought in the spirit with all his strength. He was not lazy. He didn't say, "What will be will be. God made me a promise, and I have no need to wrestle through this." God always has a way of escape for us in every situation.

> *Therefore, my dear brothers and sisters, stand firm. Let nothing move you. Always give yourselves fully to the work of the Lord, because you know that your labor in the Lord is not in vain. 1 Cor. 15:58*

> *There hath no temptation taken you but such as is common to man: but God is faithful, who will not suffer you to be tempted above that ye are able; but will with the temptation also make a way to escape, that ye may be able to bear it. 1 Cor. 10:13*

This walk is work! Give yourself wholeheartedly to the task. Why? Because you trust Him. You know that your efforts are not in vain. Jacob's labor and struggles were not in vain. He didn't know how God would act; he just believed that God would.

Living for Jesus/Yeshua isn't a walk in the park. It requires effort. There's work to be done. We must not become weary in doing good. We cannot waver from our convictions or be lazy or lackadaisical.

Ask God to open your eyes. He wants you to see. He wants you to be encouraged and to walk in boldness.

Recently, while in prayer, I saw a ring of fire surrounding our home, which comforted and encouraged me. I realized that this ring of fire was protecting us. We were safeguarded even before I was aware of the fire's presence, despite our lack of knowledge about it. That ring had been around my home long before I could see it. God is at work, even if we don't perceive it. Ask Him to open your spiritual eyes. He says you have them. Father, open the eyes of our understanding and help us see more clearly.

Ask Him to send His forces on your behalf, on behalf of your family, and on behalf of your country. He is working; He is The Commander. He is YHVH Sabaoth. The Lord of Hosts means myriads upon myriads of angels. He has a warring force; He has messenger angels, and He has protective angels. Dig into your arsenal of weapons and utilize the angelic forces that you have yet to learn to tap into.

> *See that you do not despise or think less of one of these little ones, for I say to you that their **angels** in heaven [are in the presence of and] continually look upon the face of My Father who is in heaven. Matt. 18:10*

He never refers to you as 'His adults.' Instead, He always calls you 'His little children.' Therefore, as His children, we have angels who are always beholding the face of God. They don't abandon us because we have aged or physically grown up.

Ask God for the eyes to see. However, even if you can't see, ask for faith to believe that you always have an army at your disposal. They are there as you battle in the spirit for the kingdom of God to come into your life and the lives of your family. Oh, what a God we serve who can deliver us from every situation!

Secret: *You are never too old to have guardian angels (more than one).*

On Jacob's deathbed, this is the blessing he pronounced over his son Joseph and his sons:

And he blessed Joseph, and said, God, before whom my fathers Abraham and Isaac did walk, the God which fed me all my life long unto this day, **The Angel which redeemed me from all evil,** *bless the lads; and let my name be named on them, and the name of my fathers Abraham and Isaac; and let them grow into a multitude in the midst of the earth. Gen. 48:15-16*

From womb to tomb, the angels are ever present!

Chapter 4

Angels Respond to Our Words!

What we have learned about angelic assistance in warfare is that angels are spirit beings who serve alongside us.

> *Are they not all ministering spirits, sent forth to minister for them who shall be heirs of salvation?" Heb. 1:14 KJV*

The CJB expresses it this way:

> *Aren't they all merely spirits who serve, sent out to help those whom God will deliver? Heb. 1:14*

That is us, the ones whom God is delivering: the children of God through the promises made to Abraham.

> *And I John saw these things, and heard them. And when I had heard and seen, I fell down to worship before the feet of the angel which shewed me these things. Then saith he unto me, See thou do it not: for I am thy fellowservant, and of thy brethren the prophets, and of them which keep the sayings of this book: worship God' Rev. 22:8*

The Angel is telling John to worship God, not him. We understand that the angelic family faithful to God's throne are fellow servants. Someone asked me last week if we have the authority to command angels. My response was, "I don't see that in the scriptures." They said, "Well, if they are here to minister to us, doesn't that mean we can command them?" I answered, "A fellow servant is someone who serves alongside you, working together to bring about the Kingdom of God here on earth. You and I are sisters in the Lord, serving alongside each other. I don't command you, and you do not command me. We are fellow servants, assisting each other in bringing forth the kingdom of God on this earth."

We have countless angels ready to assist us; however, we are not accustomed to asking for their help. In Chapter Three, I shared Jacob's story from the book of Jasher.

This account of Jacob and Esau describes how God sent three angels, who appeared as 2,000 fully armed warriors, to encounter Esau. This remarkable story reveals that their goal was to assist God's servant, Jacob. Their mission aimed to encourage Esau to rethink his plan to kill his brother Jacob/Israel. It is still uncertain if Jacob realizes how he was saved.

The way we saw this unfold was nothing short of amazing. The angels came in response to Jacob's wrestling. That's why they came, because of his warfare. You and I war as well; we wrestle in the spirit. Sometimes, you aren't even aware that there is a battle raging.

We see the same thing happening in the book of Daniel. The angel comes in response to Daniel's prayer. Daniel is engaged in warfare, just like Jacob was. This was not merely a simple prayer but a persistent plea for greater understanding of what he had read in the scroll of Jeremiah regarding Israel's return to the land. Daniel is desperate to understand.

Secret: Warring for your nation requires taking on principalities! You will need help!

One reason Daniel's prayers sparked such intense spiritual wrestling was that he was fighting for an entire nation. His petition was entirely selfless; it was for his people and for God's glory. Most of our personal prayers do not carry this kind of significance. However, that doesn't mean you won't be called to the same level of intensity in prayer at some point in your life.

In a sense, Jacob was doing the same thing. He was fighting not only for his own deliverance but also for the establishment of the nation of Israel according to God's will. Just as the angels showed up for Jacob, they appeared for Daniel.

We're going to explore a key section of scripture that addresses Daniel's prayer for his people. Additionally, we'll look at the scroll of Jeremiah, which inspired Daniel's appeal.

> *In the first year of Darius the son of Ahasuerus, of Median descent, who was made king over the realm of the Chaldeans-- in the first year of his reign, I, Daniel, understood from the books the number of years which, according to the word of the LORD to Jeremiah the prophet, must pass before the desolations [which had been] pronounced on Jerusalem would end; and it was seventy years. Dan. 9:1-2 Amp.*

Daniel sees this 70-year time frame, which he derives from the scroll of Jeremiah. We do the same; we examine the scriptures to understand what is to come. We need wisdom, just as Daniel did. This is what Jeremiah said:

> *This whole land will be a waste and a horror, and these nations will serve the king of Babylon seventy years. Jer. 25:11*

He makes it very clear how long Judah is going to serve Babylon. He and other prophets were sent to warn Judah numerous times, but they refused to repent or listen. God sends us warnings daily, but we, too, turn a deaf ear to His calls to repent.

> *Then when seventy years are completed, I will punish the king of Babylon and that nation, the land of the Chaldeans (Babylonia),' says the LORD, 'for their wickedness, and will make the land [of the Chaldeans] a perpetual waste. Jer. 25:12 Amp.*

Jumping down the page to Jeremiah 29:10 he says:

> *"For thus says the LORD, 'When seventy years [of exile] have been completed for Babylon, I will visit (inspect) you and keep My good promise to you, to bring you back to this place. Jer. 29:10 Amp.*

This was written by the prophet Jeremiah, which Daniel had been reading. He focuses on the Torah and the prophets, striving to understand when this captivity will end. Jeremiah instructed the captives to go to Babylon, build homes, start businesses, and raise families because their captivity was not going to be brief. He advised them to settle in and accept this period of captivity as a form of discipline. It was meant to reignite a longing for their loving, faithful God and their beloved land. We often fail to appreciate what we have until we no longer possess it.

Secret: The Word of God is filled with hidden Gems. It is the glory of God to conceal a thing, but the honor of kings to search out a matter. Pr. 25:2

Now that we understand what fueled Daniel's passion for seeking answers, we'll continue with Daniel 9.

> *So I directed my attention to the Lord God to seek Him by prayer and supplications, with fasting, sackcloth and ashes. Dan. 9:3*

Daniel has purposed to focus on Yahweh, the God of Israel. He does this by removing other distractions from his life. He is intentionally seeking God for answers. Today, we refer to this as dying to ourselves. He is silencing his fleshly desires so that his spiritual ears and eyes will be opened to God's understanding. He seeks to have the mind of Christ.

> *I prayed to the LORD my God and confessed and said, "O Lord, the great and awesome God, who keeps His covenant and extends lovingkindness toward those who love Him and keep His commandments, Dan. 9:4*

Secret: Worship is part of Warfare!

If you seek loving kindness from God, then uphold His commandments. All His promises are conditional. We do our part by loving and honoring Him as His Bride, who is preparing herself for His return. He is a covenant-keeping God and will fulfill all His promises to His family.

> *we have sinned and committed wrong, (he is including himself) and have behaved wickedly and have rebelled, turning away from Your commandments and ordinances. Dan. 9:5 Amp.*

This is exactly how we should pray for America. Daniel tells God that they have sinned. He recognizes God's righteousness and acknowledges that they deserve this punishment. When we see judgment approaching, we often wonder why. Just as Daniel said, we deserve this punishment. We have turned our backs on God. We have removed Him from our schools, our government, and, to some extent, even from our churches!

> *Further, we have not listened to and heeded Your servants the prophets, who spoke in Your name to our kings, our princes and our fathers, and to all the people of the land. Dan. 9:6*

There are more prophecies about the end times in the Old Testament than in the Book of Revelation or the entire New Testament. For the most part, American Christianity has rejected the Old Covenant. Do we have prophets today that we should be listening to? Do we even care about what they say?

> *"Righteousness belongs to You, O Lord, but to us confusion and open shame, as it is this day--to the men of Judah, to the inhabitants of Jerusalem, and to all Israel, those who are nearby and those who are far away, in all the countries to which You have driven them, because of the [treacherous] acts of unfaithfulness which they have committed against You. Dan.9:7*

Daniel says to God, they are driven all over the place, and You did that because of their sin; they deserved it. You are a righteous God, and You warned us this would happen, but we would not listen.

> *O LORD, to us belong confusion and open shame--to our kings, to our princes, and to our fathers--because we have sinned against You. To the Lord our God belong mercy and lovingkindness and forgiveness, for we have rebelled against Him; Dan. 9:8-9*

Secret: Mercy comes with repentance!

The only way we can receive mercy and forgiveness is by being obedient, confessing our sins, and once again becoming a repentant nation. America needs to repent. We must start with ourselves. We do not want to become servants to another nation. We love our freedoms.

> *and we have not obeyed the voice of the LORD our God by walking in His laws which He set before us through His servants the prophets. Yes, **all Israel** has transgressed Your law, even turning aside, not obeying Your voice; so the **curse** has been poured out on us and the oath which is written in the Law of Moses the servant of God, because we have sinned against Him. Dan. 9:10-11*

He references Deuteronomy 28, stating that if you follow my commandments, blessings will follow. However, if you disobey, curses will be your fate. It's straightforward and clear for everyone. Obedience brings longevity in the land, while disobedience subjects you to all the curses that fell upon Egypt and more.

If we are determined to remain in rebellion, we will witness things we have never seen before. Are we stubborn and desiring to place ourselves as our own God on the throne of our hearts? If we refuse to bow down and worship God, we will inevitably also experience our own captivity!

> *And He has carried out completely His [threatening] words which He had spoken against us and against our rulers [the kings, princes, and judges] who ruled us, to bring on us a great tragedy; for under the whole heaven there has not been done*

> *anything [so dreadful] like that which [He commanded and] was done to Jerusalem. Just as it is written in the Law of Moses, all this tragedy has come on us. Yet we have not **wholeheartedly begged** for forgiveness and sought the favor of the LORD our God by turning from our wickedness and paying attention to and placing value in Your truth. Dan. 9:12-13*

What does that look like? It involves begging for forgiveness, not merely tossing a few words of acknowledgment to God regarding our situation. We do not value His truth. We selectively choose what we want from God—deciding which commandments we will obey and which ones we declare are no longer relevant.

> *Therefore the LORD has kept the tragedy ready and has brought it on us, for the LORD our God is [uncompromisingly] righteous and openly just in all His works which He does--He keeps His word; and we have not obeyed His voice. "And now, O Lord our God, who brought Your people out of the land of Egypt with a mighty hand and who made for Yourself a name, as it is today-- we have sinned, we have been wicked. Dan. 9:14-15*

He reminds God of His mighty acts of deliverance in the past. Daniel has been given insight from the scroll of Jeremiah that there is a set time for this punishment. Even though God is not shortening it, they are now nearing the end of the 70-year period. He longs for God to tell him if they are about to return to Jerusalem. He yearns for his homeland, the place where God has established His name.

> *O Lord, in accordance with all Your righteous and just acts, please let Your anger and Your wrath turn away from Your city Jerusalem, Your holy mountain. Because of our sins and the wickedness of our fathers, Jerusalem and Your people have become an object of scorn and a contemptuous byword to all who are around us. Dan. 9:16*

This is God's city; it is the place on earth that He has chosen to place His name. Yet, He allowed it to become desolate because of Judah's sin.

> *Now therefore, our God, listen to (heed) the prayer of Your servant (Daniel) and his supplications, and for Your own sake let Your face shine on Your desolate sanctuary. Dan. 9:17*

He is pleading with God. This is not only for Your people but for the sake of Your Great Name! Please allow Your glory to be seen in Your city again.

> *O my God, incline Your ear and hear; open Your eyes and look at our desolations and the city which is called by Your name; for we are not presenting our supplications before You because of our own merits and righteousness, but because of Your great mercy and compassion. Dan. 9:18*

We have no merit; we have no righteousness. We do not deserve your deliverance, but because of your great mercy and compassion for us, please listen to my plea.

> *O Lord, hear! O Lord, forgive! O Lord, listen and take action! Do not delay, for Your own sake, O my God, because Your city and Your people are called by Your name." Dan. 9:19*

The Angel Gabriel Brings an Answer:

> *While I was still speaking and praying, and confessing my sin and the sin of my people Israel, and presenting my supplication before the LORD my God in behalf of the holy mountain of my God, while I was still speaking in prayer and extremely exhausted, the man Gabriel, whom I had seen in the earlier vision, came to me about the time of the evening sacrifice. Dan. 9:20-21*

Daniel prayed until he was exhausted. Remember, Jacob wrestled all night. This is a battle, a war.

> *He instructed me and he talked with me and said, "O Daniel, I have now come to give you insight and wisdom and understanding. Dan. 9:22*

Daniel is praying for wisdom, insight, and understanding. That's what we should be praying for. Pay attention to who is bringing this wisdom. It is being brought by an **angelic being**, a fellow servant who has been battling alongside Daniel, even though he had no knowledge of it.

> *At the beginning of your supplications, the command [to give you an answer] was issued, and I have come to tell you, for you are highly regarded and greatly beloved. Therefore consider the message and begin to understand the [meaning of the] vision. Dan. 9:23*

Secret: Angels are sent to bring you wisdom in the war.

A commandment was issued from Heaven at the very moment Daniel began to pray. Yahweh sent an angel to bring the wisdom and understanding that Daniel so desperately sought. Angels are sent to provide wisdom to both you and me. What occurs when YOU start to pray?

Secret: Sometimes, you get more than you bargained for when the angels appear!

The angel is speaking to Daniel. He tells him that his people will return, but he provides Daniel with far more information than he ever requested or anticipated. The angel starts to explain the seventy weeks of Messiah.

> *"Seventy weeks [of years, or 490 years] have been decreed for your people and for your holy city (Jerusalem), to finish the transgression, to make an end of sins, to make atonement (reconciliation) for wickedness, to bring in everlasting righteousness (right-standing with God), to seal up vision and prophecy and prophet, and to anoint the Most Holy Place. So you*

are to know and understand that from the issuance of the command to restore and rebuild Jerusalem until [the coming of] the Messiah (the Anointed One), the Prince, there will be seven weeks [of years] and sixty-two weeks [of years]; it will be built again, with [a city] plaza and moat, even in times of trouble. Dan. 9:24-25

Secret: Revelations that are not understood may arise from your spiritual warfare!

The temple will be rebuilt, and not only that, the much-awaited MESSIAH will arrive! Whoa… Daniel, who is simply asking when his people will return to the land, is now being given a coded message that he will never understand. Even today, scholars who believe they have figured this out could still be mistaken.

Believers all over the earth are currently awaiting the return of our Great God and King, the Son of God, Yeshuah Mashiach. What would you do if a man from another realm appeared during your prayer and began giving you secret messages about how, when, and where the Messiah will return? Thank God that Daniel wrote this all down for future generations. This is why I encourage everyone to document every spiritual experience.

We read in the books of Ezra and Nehemiah that the Temple was rebuilt during very difficult times. Since our focus is not on the seventy weeks of Daniel but rather on angelic assistance, I won't delve into an explanation of the timing here. I have done that on some of my YouTube videos.

The angel reveals to Daniel that his people will return, and the temple will be rebuilt. This is what is on Daniel's heart. The angel has been sent with a message to reassure him that what he is reading and understanding is correct.

There is a bonus in this message from the angel. Not only is the city and temple set to be rebuilt, but the Messiah will come, too. Daniel wasn't even praying about this. How often do angels bring us messages to reassure you and me, and at times, they even provide us with bonus information?

> *Then after the sixty-two weeks [of years] the Anointed One will be cut off [and denied His Messianic kingdom] and have nothing [and no one to defend Him], and the people of the [other] prince who is to come will destroy the city and the sanctuary. Its end will come with a flood; even to the end there will be war; desolations are determined. And he will enter into a binding and irrevocable covenant with the many for one week (seven years), but in the middle of the week he will stop the sacrifice and grain offering [for the remaining three and one-half years]; and on the wing of abominations will come one who makes desolate, even until the complete destruction, one that is decreed, is poured out on the one who causes the horror." Dan. 9:26-27*

So, at this point, Daniels is saying, "What? What does all this mean?" The angel has not only answered Daniel's prayer but has gone far beyond what Daniel had expected.

So, in prayer and spiritual warfare, who comes to answer Daniel but an angel? This is "Angelic Intervention in Spiritual Warfare." They arrive to inform us of what is going to happen or what is currently happening. Sometimes, we don't even grasp what we've heard.

That is why we keep a journal and write it down. Daniel recorded it so you and I would have what the angel told him, even if he didn't fully grasp it. We see this in the book of Revelation as well. John documented everything he witnessed, though that doesn't mean he understood it. I have years of journals dating back to 1975. I am often amazed at what I have been told in prayer as I flip through the years of my writings.

I'd like you to notice one more thing. So, we will continue on to Chapter 10 of Daniel.

> *(In the third year of Cyrus king of Persia a message was revealed to Daniel, who was named Belteshazzar; and the message was true and it referred to great conflict (warfare, misery). And he understood the message and had an understanding of the vision. Dan. 10:1*

So, Daniel understands this vision.

> *In those days I, Daniel, had been mourning for three entire weeks. I ate no tasty food, nor did any meat or wine enter my mouth; and I did not anoint (refresh, groom) myself at all for the full three weeks. On the twenty-fourth day of the first month, as I was on the bank of the great river Hiddekel [which is the Tigris], I raised my eyes and looked, and behold, there was a certain man dressed in linen, whose loins were girded with [a belt of] pure gold of Uphaz. (a famous gold region) Dan. 10:2-5 Amp.*

This is yet another angelic being who resembles a man. It is the same situation we saw with Jacob, who felt as if he were wrestling with a man. The same is true for Joshua. Just before they are ready to enter Jericho, who appears? The commander of the Army of Hosts. This is the Lord of Heaven's armies, Yeshua. He appears as a man. This is how God relates to humankind: He manifests in human form.

Yeshua came in the flesh, allowing us to relate to him. He was tempted just like we are. There is nothing we experience that he hasn't already faced.

Secret: Some of God's angels are frightening.

Daniel described this angel in detail. It is not unusual for fire to be associated with God's Kingdom. Remember, our God Himself is a consuming fire!

> *His body also was like beryl [with a golden luster], his face had the appearance of **lightning**, his eyes were like **flaming torches**,*

> *his arms and his feet like the gleam of burnished bronze, and the sound of his words was like the noise of a multitude [of people or the roaring of the sea]. And I, Daniel, alone saw the vision [of this heavenly being], for the men who were with me did not see the vision; nevertheless, a great panic overwhelmed them, so they ran away to hide themselves. Dan. 10:6-7 Amp.*

They didn't see, but Daniel did. This happens frequently. Elisha witnessed the angel armies when his servant didn't.

The first time I visited Zion's Hope (The Holy Land Experience) in Orlando, Florida, we attended a historical presentation of the Tabernacle service. I came out of the Tabernacle and said to those who were with me, "That was amazing! The special effects they used in there were incredible!" We had just witnessed a presentation of a priest offering incense in the Tabernacle. Those with me replied, "What are you talking about?" I asked, "What about that huge angel standing behind the priest who was burning the incense?" They all replied, "We don't know what you're talking about. We didn't see any of that."

I had seen a colossal angel towering over the altar of incense behind the priest. It reached the height of the tabernacle and was enormous in size. No one had seen this angel but me. I thought it was some form of computer-generated image I had encountered. However, that was long before we had easy access to that kind of technology. Not everyone will see the same thing.

The same thing happened to Paul on the road to Damascus. No one saw anything but him. Sometimes, you will see things that I don't see. My husband, Ben, often sees things that I don't.

Returning to Daniel.

> *So I was left alone and saw this great vision; yet no strength was left in me, for my normal appearance turned to a deathly pale, and I grew weak and faint [with fright]. Then I heard the sound*

> *of his words; and when I heard the sound of his words, I fell on my face in a deep sleep, with my face toward the ground. Dan. 10:8-9 Amp.*

In Genesis 15, Abraham fell into a deep sleep when God walked through the pieces to establish the covenant for the land. Daniel experiences something similar; he finds himself in the presence of an angel and also falls into a deep sleep. I believe that the human body cannot endure the presence of these angelic beings very well, and perhaps falling asleep allows them to minister to us while we are in a state of slumber.

> *Then behold, a hand touched me and set me unsteadily on my hands and knees. Dan. 10:10*

So he can't stand completely up yet. He is on hands and his knees.

> *So he said to me, "O Daniel, you highly regarded and greatly beloved man, understand the words that I am about to say to you and stand upright, for I have now been sent to you." And while he was saying this word to me, I stood up trembling. Dan. 10:11*

Secret: The presence of angels can make you weak!

Stand upright is the same thing the angel says to John in Revelations more than once.

> *Then said he unto me, Fear not, Daniel: for from the first day that thou didst set thine heart to understand, and to chasten thyself before thy God, thy words were heard, and **I am come for thy words**. Dan. 10:12 KJV*

Secret: Angels come for your Words!

The phrase, "I have come because of your WORDS," brings me to tears. That illustrates the power of **our** words. They prompt the angels to respond. This is more than a little significant! Our words can activate angels. Words that align with God's will and purpose will activate angels!

How important is it for you and me to be speaking what God says about every situation?

Words are weapons. Words move mountains. Words can kill or bring life. Prayer and repentance summon the angels. Your words call forth angels!

As the angel continues speaking to Daniel, he reveals the extent of the warfare that has taken place in the heavens to deliver this message to Daniel.

> *But the prince of the kingdom of Persia was standing in opposition to me for twenty-one days. Then, behold, Michael, one of the chief [of the celestial] princes, came to help me, for I had been left there with the kings of Persia. Dan. 10:13*

So, he is fighting against principalities, trying to deliver this message to Daniel. That is what angels do for us. They wage war against principalities—wicked, evil forces in the heavenly realms over earthly kingdoms. A spirit was controlling the country of Persia, opposing the angel assigned to bring a message to Daniel. Remember, this message also contained coded information about the coming of the Messiah, which Satan has been watching for since Genesis three, where he was told that the seed of the woman would crush his head!

> *Now I have come to make you understand what will happen to your people in the latter days, for the vision is in regard to the days yet to come." Dan. 10:14*

Angels come in response to your words, to your warfare. Angels bring understanding and tell you what is about to come! Awesome!

I need to understand, do you? Angels are working and present whether you see them or not. They are here to assist us on this journey. We are facing troubling times. Do not forget the weapons in your arsenal for the fight. Ask for angelic assistance as you face these coming days. You are going to need it.

Sometimes, I feel like I'm walking between raindrops of judgment, dodging them as the Father guides me. It's almost like avoiding landmines, and He shows us where to step to stay safe. Soon, it will pour, and our only hope is that we are in the Father and He is in us. He is our protection, and He WILL send angels in response to our words.

> *Therefore, confess your sins to one another [your false steps, your offenses], and pray for one another, that you may be healed and restored. The heartfelt and persistent prayer of a righteous man (believer) can accomplish much [when put into action and made effective by God--it is dynamic and can have tremendous power]. Jas. 5:16 Amp*

Secret: Your words, prayers, and warfare hold tremendous power!

> *Confess your faults one to another, and pray one for another,* ***that ye may be healed****. The effectual fervent prayer of a righteous man availeth much. Jas. 5:16 KJV*

For those of us looking for healing, it requires confessing our sins. It is about getting our hearts right.

Before we begin interceding for others, it is wise to clear our hearts first. We should examine ourselves to see if we have any sins or areas that we need to submit to God. What might we be walking in that could hinder our prayers? And how fervent are our prayers? How much time are we willing to spend in God's presence? Will the angels respond because of your words?

The Bible says that they do. Whether you see angels or not, they are there, and they are part of your armor, just as much as the helmet of salvation, the breastplate of righteousness, and the sword of the Spirit. They are here to minister to us, the heirs of salvation. It is all part of your arsenal. They are fellow servants, warring alongside us.

I have seen some things in the arsenal of God that are far more frightening than anything the devil has to offer. If Satan can devise terrifying things, don't you think that God is even more capable of this than he is? Our Supreme, magnificent God frightens the devil!

Chapter 5

It's a War of Words!

Secret: Our Words are Weapons.

This Battle is A War of Words. Words are Containers That Hold Power.

Remember that the angels came because of Daniel's words. That is precisely the kind of response we desire. Our words activate angels. If our words contradict God or His Word, the angels will not be inclined to appear. Hopefully, we will develop a profound understanding of how our words affect the direction of our lives and our place in the earth. Many believers are unaware of the immense power that resides within our words. According to Scripture, angels respond to what we say. Our words can serve as powerful weapons; they are containers that we can fill with explosive ingredients or with junk.

> *Then said he unto me, Fear not, Daniel: for from the first day that thou didst set thine heart to understand, and to chasten thyself before thy God, thy words were heard, and **I am come for thy words**. Dan. 10:12*

> *Bless the LORD, ye his angels, that excel in strength, that do his commandments, hearkening unto the voice of his word. Ps. 103:20*

The angels hearken to God's Word when we speak what God speaks. In the next chapter, we'll observe two women in a continuing conflict. Both have words that produce results. Some words are for good, and others are for evil.

Before we go there, we need to consider what's required of a warrior in the kingdom of God. Every military soldier goes through boot camp in preparation for war. They receive standard equipment and learn to use their weapons correctly. For God's Army here on earth, there is little time left to prepare for the battles ahead. We have been given the power of our words, which are more potent in the spirit than bullets are in the natural. This book is part of your preparation. It is written to empower you to use all the spiritual weapons that have been issued to you, including how to call for backup: "Angelic Assistance!"

In Chapter One, I shared a bit about the power of angelic assistance in warfare. We considered that if only one-third of the angels fell in rebellion against God, it meant that two-thirds remained loyal to His throne. We also explored the possibility that since angels are created beings, God may have made many more after the fall of the rebellious ones. However, I realize this is debatable.

We are engaged in an invisible spiritual war that is becoming increasingly visible daily. The enemy is emboldened and rarely even conceals his actions. We're fighting a life-and-death battle for our loved ones' souls and our own well-being. The good news is that YOU were created to be a warrior! Every believer in Yeshua/Jesus should be actively resisting the Kingdom of Darkness.

We witnessed Jacob wrestling with the angel throughout the night, ultimately prevailing. James explains how that occurred:

> *confess your sins to one another [your false steps, your offenses], and pray for one another, that you may be healed and restored. The **heartfelt and persistent prayer** of a righteous man (believer) can accomplish much [when put into action and made effective by God—it is dynamic and can have tremendous power]. James 5:16 Amp*

Part of prayer involves confession and repentance. This is clearly illustrated in "The Lord's Prayer," where we are encouraged to seek forgiveness and to forgive others as well.

And forgive us our debts, as we forgive our debtors. Matt. 6:12

It's those fervent and heartfelt prayers that truly connect with God. Not the ones where you bow your head and say, "Bless so and so," then casually move on.

As we learn to engage deeply with the things of God—serious and fervent prayer—angelic beings will attend. We don't have to ask; they begin to manifest. When we pray, they respond to our words. We have witnessed this often in our private and group prayer meetings.

The angels have received assignments and will occasionally make themselves known. This isn't something we conjure up or imagine; it happens according to God's sovereignty.

The angels are working on our behalf. We are part of their family. Both we and they are created beings. Humankind exists in this tangible realm while they reside in the invisible kingdom. The scriptures reveal their ability to transition from the invisible to the visible. They possess the power to navigate both realms, which we, as physical beings, cannot do.

In Genesis 18, before the destruction of Sodom and Gomorrah, we see the two angels arriving with Yahweh Himself. As they approach Abraham's tent, all three appear to be in human form. They linger with him and share a meal. They eat solid food and are present in fleshly bodies that function just like humans, including consuming food during their earthly visit.

They ate, drank, and talked with Abraham. The Scriptures tell us these were supernatural beings engaging in ordinary human activities. These angels came in response to the outcry against the wickedness of Sodom.

Then the Lord said, "The outcry against Sodom and Gomorrah is so great and their sin so grievous that I will go down and see if what they have done is as bad as the outcry that has reached me. If not, I will know." Gen. 18:20-21 NIV

The Word doesn't disclose who was uttering these cries against Sodom; however, the inhabitants were well-known for their cruel treatment of any foreigner or visitor to the city.

In the ancient Near East, the Hebrews had an understanding that there were two Yahwehs.* This is evidenced in Daniel 7:9-14, where the Ancient of Days is depicted seated on His throne, and one like a human being comes in the clouds, crowned and granted kingship. Therefore, the belief was in an invisible Yahweh and one who is visible.

In my view, that belief paves the way for Jesus's incarnation. If Jesus/Yeshua is God in the flesh and He and the Father are one, that represents a God who is seen and one who is invisible. Jesus is seen on earth, and the Father is invisible in heaven!

It is a given that God is invisible. However, there are instances in the scriptures when He appears in human form, as seen in the example above with Abraham.

It's easy to understand that God and even angels can transition between realms, whether seen or unseen. In this chapter, we explore angelic intervention in our earthly battles. Angels are influenced by our words. By the way, evil fallen angels are also moved by your words. That is why our words are so powerful and must be guarded.

Secret: *Not only are good angels moved by your words, but so are the evil ones!*

Many believers come to faith without realizing that they have enlisted in a war. Instead, they are told to walk down an aisle, pray, and secure their ticket to heaven because God has a plan for their lives. Well, He does have a plan for your life, and it includes spiritual warfare.

*Michael S. Heiser, Unseen Realm, Lexham Press, 2015, pg.133.

There is an ever present invisible battle for your soul. That's how valuable you are to both God and the devil. They are both after your soul.

When we commit to follow Jesus/Yeshua, it signifies an all-or-nothing allegiance. It means you are completely devoted to Him. We become His servants, and He is our Master. We are here to carry out His wishes and to be among His soldiers. He's the General, giving the orders, and we who have ears to hear are the soldiers in His earthly army. He's provided us with an instruction manual, yet most of us prefer to skip reading the rule book, the Bible.

As a little girl in Sunday School, I learned the song "Onward Christian Soldiers." It never registered in my young mind that there was a real war; I thought it was just a cute little song. We marched to the music and stomped our feet with each step and beat. It was simply a fun activity for us. The truth of those words held no meaning for me.

So, even if no one has ever told you that you were in a war, and you're just starting to realize the seriousness of your commitment, there's still good news. God created YOU to battle, to wage war. You were born to fight, to stand strong. You are stronger than you can ever imagine.

"We sang another song, 'I'm in the Lord's Army." No one ever explained those words, either. What did that mean?"

You are a flesh-and-blood being created in God's own image; Satan despises you for that. You were designed to take dominion in this earthly realm. We, as humankind, are meant to rule on this planet. Satan has attempted to usurp that authority, but his actions are unlawful. Dominion was given to Adam, not to a fallen angel. Jesus' death paid the price for our fallen nature and restored our original authority to rule. The work of the cross has liberated us from Satan's control.

Here's a side note: Never forget this! The earth is to be ruled solely by mankind, not by Satan, an angel, or an alien. Just in case a strange creature appears and claims to have created you. You know who the father of lies is.

> *Look, I have given you authority over all the power of the enemy...Luk. 10:19 NLT*

Our assignment is to enforce the victory that Jesus won on the cross and usher in "The Kingdom of God." Most of us haven't grasped that. We were thrilled to receive our golden ticket to heaven when we were saved. What more did we need?

In truth, we were delivered from the "kingdom of darkness," the devil's grip on our souls. We were rescued from the law of sin and death that came as a result of Adam's treason against God in the Garden of Eden. The penalty for our sin was eternal death. Jesus took that penalty and nailed it to the cross, erasing the penalty of death for us and ensuring our eternal life. We do not have to die. While our fleshly bodies will cease to function, our souls will live on in the presence of God forever.

Satan's desire for all humanity is "eternal death." He despises us. We are created in the image of God. His very name, YHVH (Yahweh), is inscribed on our DNA strands. *

Trust me, if the devil can find a way to corrupt humanity's DNA, he will. He doesn't play fairly. He embodies deception and will trick you in any way he can. He never follows the rules.

Secret: God's name is on your DNA!

We are not only in a battle with a real-life enemy, but we also have an obligation to fight. We are enlisted whether we like it or not. God has equipped us according to Eph. 6, and we also have powerful, continuous support from our angelic brothers. We possess the strength to stand firm and even to reclaim ground for the Kingdom of God. Our presence on

*www.delightfulknowledge.com/hidden-name-of-creator-in-your-dna

this earth should make a difference in the spiritual realm and in the lives of others.

> *Put on the whole armour of God, that ye may be able to stand against the wiles of the devil. For we wrestle not against flesh and blood, but against principalities, against powers, against the rulers of the darkness of this world, against spiritual wickedness in high places. Wherefore take unto you the whole armour of God, that ye may be able to withstand in the evil day, and having done all, to stand. Eph. 6:11-13*

If we are not stirring up the kingdom of darkness with our message and prayers, then we aren't fulfilling our role. Satan's time is limited, and he is aware of it. Revelation 12 tells us he is furious. That's because those who pray disrupt his plans, and he has only so much time left. He is bound by time, just like we are. God exists outside of time; He can be as patient as He chooses. That's not the case for the enemy. He has been assigned a limited timeframe to carry out his agenda, and that time is running out!

If you are spiritually at war, you are compelling the devil to stop and clean up small messes here and there. It doesn't matter if you simply place a little stumbling block in his path by praying in the spirit about something. Any hindrance you create against the kingdom of darkness is advantageous. Together, our small disturbances in his kingdom add up.

To stay strong and ready for battle, it's crucial to reflect periodically on the beginnings of your faith and recall the joy of your salvation. Demonic spiritual attacks are aimed at stealing our joy.

In recent years, we as a nation have witnessed an increase in deaths, even among young people. The sadness will be overwhelming if we do not stay rooted in God's Word. God's Word is life; it restores our joy and reenergizes us. If the devil can keep you in a state of sadness, you'll become ineffective in your spiritual warfare. He aims to keep you distracted so he doesn't have to deal with you. If you do not resist, he will lead you into despair and depression, and at that point, he has won.

> *Submit yourselves, therefore, to God. Resist the devil, and he will flee from you. Jm.4:7*

One of the best ways to submit to God and make the devil flee is through worship. The devil despises our worship of God. Stay rooted in the Word, especially the Psalms. King David understood how to lift himself out of despair by praising God. Just look at Psalm 91. We find refuge in the shadow of the Almighty God. Talk about angelic assistance! If you stumble, the angels are there to lift you up. Praise the Lord! With a long life, He will satisfy you. I'm personally holding on to that promise. I want to live to see the coming of the Lord, and I imagine you do too.

Secret: Remembering the day you were saved strengthens your resolve for the upcoming battle.

Revisiting the core of our faith rekindles the joy of our salvation. This is essential. Never forget the moment you gave your heart to the Lord.

What happened that day? Oh, all our burdens were lifted. We entrusted all our concerns to him and knew everything would be okay. The earthly consequences of all your sins didn't vanish, but the eternal consequences completely disappeared. Hallelujah. Suddenly, you were free from the clutches of the devil and his plans for your life. For whom the Father sets free is free indeed, and where the Spirit of the Lord is, there is liberty.

> *If the Son therefore shall make you free, ye shall be free indeed. Jn.8:36*

We had nothing to offer God at that moment but our brokenness, and He said, "Come on, child, I love you. I'll take you just as you are."

The longer we serve God, the more we believe we have something to offer. Everything we possess, our very existence, is solely by His divine plan and purpose for our lives. He's the one who empowers us and gives us the strength to move forward in fulfilling what He expects of us. He is our source.

Was there a significant change in your life when you were saved? If you can't recall the beauty of the born-again experience, pause and pray right now. Surrender your will to follow Jesus wholeheartedly. Then, note this day as your new beginning.

Ask yourself these questions: "Did you truly commit to living for God, or did you simply agree that believing in Him to secure your place in heaven sounded like a good idea? Did you fall in love with Him and surrender completely on that day? Did you make Him your master? Did you decide to seek His guidance in every aspect of your life? If not, then why not start now?

If you didn't sell out that day, it's time to say, "Here I am, God. It's all or nothing!"

Are you still on the throne of your own life? Are you considering Him in your relationships, finances, health, and future? Or are those still all your own decisions? Are you still calling all the shots and doing whatever you want?

Yeshua is either the master of all, or He is not your master at all! You decide. These conditions are prerequisites to aligning with the Commander, who should be making all the decisions.

Secret: If You Ask God More Questions, You Get More Answers

Consult Him about your daily decisions. You can talk to Him throughout the day in brief moments and longer conversations. Commit to spending time in His Word; it's His love letter to you. Ask Him for wisdom and understanding; seek His guidance in teaching you. Trust Him for those AH-Ha moments; these are precious times when all the puzzle pieces start to fit together. Pose questions to Him. How did this happen? Why did this happen? What do you want me to learn from this? Converse with Him. He responds to your words.

When I discover a new biblical truth, I reflect on it repeatedly until I start to think, "Well, if that's true... then this must also be true. Now I understand how everything fits together! Isn't that exciting?"

Sometimes, he'll say something to us that we don't fully understand. We just know we're witnessing something. If we continue to question, it will become clear. Eventually, we can express what we're receiving from the Spirit. It takes time to recognize new truths and activate them in our lives.

In this spiritual battle, we must be open to realizing that we may have learned falsehoods. We can't be so sure that we have a handle on what God is saying that we can't change when new revelations surface.

> *Let this mind be in you, which was also in Christ Jesus: Phil. 2:5*
>
> *......For out of the abundance of the heart the mouth speaketh. Matt. 12:34*

"Let this mind be in you, which was also in Christ Jesus," refers to adopting the same mindset or thinking that Christ possessed. Whatever is in our minds will eventually come out of our mouths through our **words**! It manifests in our conversations. It reveals the truth of who we really are and what's hidden in our hearts.

When Paul says to let this mind be in you, he is referring to how Jesus, as God, was willing to give up His glory. He humbled Himself by becoming a man (God in the flesh) and accepting a brutal death on the cross. Jesus surrendered Himself as a demonstration of complete selfless love, lowering Himself to show that love. He stands as the supreme example of selflessness and humility. Jesus tells us that no one has greater love than to give his life for others.

> *....Greater love has no one than this: to lay down one's life for one's friends." John 15:13*

If you keep looking at Him, you will become like Him.

> *Herein is our love made perfect, that we may have boldness in the day of judgment: because as he is, so are we in this world. 1 Jn 4:17*

The Apostle Paul challenges us to think this way—to be willing to humble ourselves for the benefit of others. That's how we can share the same mindset and maintain the same love. He urges us to prioritize the interests and purposes of others for their good. When a soldier goes into battle, he is willing to sacrifice his life for his country. We, too, have a country, but it is not of this world.

How often do we engage in activities that bring us joy without considering others? If we think like Yeshua/Jesus, our bodies will follow our thoughts.

Soldiers operate as a cohesive unit in a war zone, watching out for each other. The battle is not solely about you; it's about the mission.

If your mind is aligned with God's Word, your body will not dictate your actions; Instead, your spirit will guide them. What we place in our hearts and minds determines how we will succeed in this battle. If we don't renew our minds, our bodies will control our actions, and actions have consequences.

What Warfare is not!

Warfare is not about praying to escape a crisis that you created for yourself. People voice this all the time. They say, "Boy, I'm really in a battle," yet it is often a situation they brought upon themselves. They usually can't see that because they haven't truly let go of their ego. It's always easier to blame someone or something else.

The quicker we learn to say, "I'm guilty; I messed up," the quicker God will forgive us and make things right. He did it for David. David was an adulterer and a murderer, but he had a heart willing to admit his wrongs, and he was quick to repent. God loved that about him. He may have sinned, but he was quick to seek forgiveness. It's a quality we all should learn.

Warfare involves loving and praying for others while trusting God to meet your own needs as you intercede. It's a matter of faith

If you are fighting a personal battle repeatedly, then it is time for the loops in your life to be closed. They are like the same recordings playing over and over. We used to call this a broken record. We think we've stopped the music, only to have it start up again. If you never address the source of the problem, it will never be resolved. It's time to shut down these strongholds. How many times have you fought the same battle? You don't want to keep fighting for the same hill repeatedly.

If you keep thinking you'll deal with an issue someday but never do, admit it: you are a procrastinator. No one can make you a better soldier in the Kingdom of God; that responsibility lies with you. So, grab your journal, sit down, and take some time. Ask God, "What's in my life that I keep battling and never achieving victory over? Why? What's the reason? Is this demonic? Is this generational? Is this something I have never been willing to confront? God, please help me to understand. Teach me." He loves to teach you.

Fasting is an excellent way to break strongholds. If you're struggling to receive answers, silence your flesh so you can listen with spiritual ears. Ask God if unresolved issues are blocking your ability to hear His voice. What are these issues, and how can you overcome them? Being honest with yourself and controlling your flesh makes you more attuned to the spiritual realm.

Remember: Angels Respond to YOUR Prayers (words).

Out of the abundance of your heart, your mouth will speak. You want your **words** to be God's words. The angels hearken to the voice of the Lord when you speak His words or when they are directly spoken by Him. They will respond when you speak in accordance with the Word. The Host of

Heaven is immense. His angel armies are innumerable. There is plenty to go around, and they aren't bothered by your personal struggles. They are already present. If you need assistance in a battle, ask God to send help.

When we think about Spiritual Warfare, we often first consider prayer. Prayer is a form of warfare; however, spiritual warfare encompasses more than just prayer. I'm sure we can all agree that prayer takes many different forms. The single most important factor in Spiritual Warfare is your walk! The way you live each moment of every day reflects your walk. How are you living? Are you striving to move in righteousness?

Warfare also involves rebuking the enemy and commanding him to leave or cease his activities. Warfare declares God's Word and His superior authority over the devil. We are proclaiming what God has already said. Sometimes, warfare includes performing deliverance by casting out evil spirits or influences.

As sons and daughters of the King, and those called to be priests unto our God, we make decrees and declarations. Naturally, these decrees are pronouncements that align with what God's Word has already proclaimed. We declare what He has declared.

In the Book of Revelation, we see that the prayers of believers are stored in golden vials in heaven. The final judgments on earth are the bowl judgments. The **angels** mix our prayers with fire from the heavenly altar and incense. They are poured out upon the earth as part of the final judgment.

> *And when he had taken the book, the four beasts and four and twenty elders fell down before the Lamb, having every one of them harps and golden vials full of odors, which are the prayers of saints. Rev. 5:9*

For those who believe their prayers aren't being heard, you are wrong. Your prayers are acknowledged and kept in heaven. You may not receive an answer to your specific prayer in your lifetime. Many patriarchs in

Scripture died without seeing their promises fulfilled. Many of their prayers were answered for the generations that came after their death.

Our prayers are rooted in faith. Just like the angels that we may not see, the answers to our prayers are already in existence. The answers may already be on their way. Just because you don't see your answer immediately doesn't mean that tomorrow isn't the day it will manifest.

Often, the key is learning to wait on the Lord. Waiting on the Lord is an active position. Spending time with Him, sitting before Him, and listening for His voice requires time. We shouldn't be anxious or try to be "the great fixer" on our own. We're not meant to control our own destiny in our own way. Remove yourself from the throne of your life and give Yeshua/Jesus that position. He is the King. As much as you may want to call all the shots while serving God, you don't have that privilege. When you do that, you are not serving God; you are serving self!

Trusting God with our children and loved ones is challenging for us. Many of us are natural rescuers and fixers. Watching those we love struggle is hard, so we do everything we can to prevent that. Often, we don't even think to ask the father, "What's your plan for this person?" Sometimes, we must get out of God's way. Surrender your grand ideas, dreams, and aspirations, and allow God to be God for the other person. Step aside and let God work! Speak what God says about that person, not what you see, but what God says.

We have established that angels respond to your words. Your words are indeed powerful. They invoke the presence of angelic beings. I remind you that God has two families: the one we see and the one we don't see. Both we and the angels are created beings. Humans are especially blessed because we are created in the image of God Himself.

We are the only flesh creatures on Earth who possess a mouth and the intelligence to speak. With our words, we can attract things to ourselves, whether good or bad.

> *"A good man out of the good treasure of his heart bringeth forth that which is good; and an evil man out of the evil treasure of his heart bringeth forth that which is evil: for of the abundance of the heart his mouth speaketh." Luke 6;45*

The things that dwell abundantly in our hearts are the very things that eventually come out of our mouths. Sometimes, we say things that are the exact opposite of what we desire or what God wants for our lives. This occurs when we express negative words about ourselves and those we love. We speak unfavorably about our children, jobs, bosses, homes, and even our financial situations. Are you condemning yourself with your own words? Are you opening a portal for the enemy to enter your life?

> *Out of the same mouth proceedeth blessing and cursing. My brethren, these things ought not so to be. James 3:10*

When others speak negatively about these things, do you find yourself agreeing with them? Or are you bold enough to challenge what is being implied? If you remain silent, they will assume you agree. By doing this, you become a second witness to the enemy. The scriptures tell us that every word is established in the presence of two or three witnesses. Trust me, you don't want to align yourself with the devil on anything.

Secret: Satan thrives on iniquity; don't nourish him with your WORDS of agreement!

Our words are a tremendous gift from our Creator. Our words can be weapons. So, when we engage in battle, we use words. As you speak, your voice creates vibrations that travel through the air. They enter the atmosphere, affecting everything that exists in and on the Earth. When we speak God's words, it always produces results that will benefit God's Kingdom.

> *So shall my word be that goeth forth out of my mouth: it shall not return unto me void, but it shall accomplish that which I please, and it shall prosper in the thing whereto I sent it. Is. 55:11*

When you speak the Word of God, it will always accomplish what He intended. His Word never returns to Him empty. Wonderful things are already prepared for us in the spiritual realm, including husbands, wives, finances, homes, healings, peace, wisdom, victory, and many other blessings. All of these are drawn from the spiritual realm to us through our faith and our words.

> *Set a watch, O LORD, before my mouth; keep the door of my lips. Ps. 141:3*

> *You are snared by the words of your mouth; You are taken by the words of your mouth. Pr. 6:2*

In this war of words, make sure you are saying what God is saying for you and those around you. What is He saying about your city, your nation, and the world? Avoid voicing what you do not wish to see. Your agreement empowers the forces of darkness when your words align with the enemy.

It is a biblical principle that it takes two to agree to establish a matter. Don't give the devil a second witness by agreeing with him. Align your words with God's instead of the devil's. Avoid repeating what the media says if you don't want to give it more power. Words hold power. Words are weapons!

Chapter 6

Yahweh Sabaoth (Lord of Host)

The earlier chapters provide an overview of spiritual warfare and its critical importance in each of our lives. We examined the importance of truly dedicating ourselves to serving God to succeed in the battle against the "spirit of death." Satan's goal is to take away the precious gift of eternal life from you and your loved ones.

Remember, both God and Satan are after your soul. You are truly valuable to both kingdoms. Satan desires to destroy anything that reflects the image of God, which is **you!** Meanwhile, Jesus came to give life, and that more abundantly.

We serve a supernatural God, and what He has done for others, He WILL do for YOU!

> *I will praise thee; for I am fearfully and wonderfully made: marvellous are thy works; and that my soul knoweth right well. Pd. 139:14*

You are an amazement! Unique in every way, chosen by God.

Now, let's delve into how angels fight for God's people. This will genuinely strengthen your faith!

It's vital to have confidence that you're not fighting alone. In the days ahead, you will encounter new enemies. These are the last days! We are facing foes that have never been heard of on Earth before our time: things like AI, drones, aliens, clones, colonies on Mars, and world wars with unimaginable weapons. However, we have the same God, and He remains unchanged—yesterday, today, and forever. If He sent angels to defeat whole human armies, He can and will do it again.

Hopefully, your appetite has been stirred to seek more than just a lackluster relationship with the true and living God. The Apostle Paul prayed for our spiritual eyes to be enlightened. He wouldn't have asked for that if it were not possible. Decide right now whether it is possible for you. Tell the Lord, "I want more!"

> *The eyes of your understanding being enlightened; that ye may know what is the hope of his calling, and what the riches of the glory of his inheritance in the saints, Eph. 1:18*

In the book of First Samuel, Hannah, one of God's handmaidens, desired "more." She exemplifies the virtues of perseverance and determination. During her time of relentless torment, she calls upon God and His angelic forces to stand against those whose intent was to bring her grief.

Some of you may already know this story but might not have seen it in the light I'm about to share. Hannah is the very first person in the scriptures to refer to God as "Yahweh Sabaoth," or "Lord of Hosts." Why is that?

The Strong's Concordance defines the term "host" as a great army ready at God's command. "Lord of Hosts" is one of God's names and appears 235 times in the Bible. The very first instance is in the story of Hannah. Hannah faced an ongoing struggle with an adversary and with what seemed to be a curse of barrenness.

Since Hannah was the first biblical character to call God by this name, "Lord of Host," where did she gain this knowledge? How did she know to address God with that title? What insight did she possess that others at that time lacked? After she uses this title, it is repeated 234 times by others throughout the Word of God. Hannah, who becomes the mother of Samuel, had tapped into an understanding of God that was not yet recognized. She seemingly understood that God had a military force and that she had access to it.

The story begins with Elkanah, Hannah's husband, and his two wives embarking on their annual journey to one of Israel's feasts. His wife Peninnah has children, but Hannah is barren.

> *And this man went up out of his city yearly to worship and to sacrifice unto the LORD of hosts in Shiloh. And the two sons of Eli, Hophni and Phinehas, the priests of the LORD, were there. And when the time was that Elkanah offered, he gave to Peninnah his wife, and to all her sons and her daughters, portions: But unto Hannah he gave a worthy portion; for he loved Hannah: but the LORD had shut up her womb. And **her adversary** also **provoked** her sore, for to make her **fret**, because the LORD had shut up her womb. 1 Sam. 1:4-6*

We're told that the Lord had shut Hannah's womb. This theme appears consistently throughout Scripture. When there is more than one wife, the more beloved wife is often barren, while the other is fertile. However, we will discover that there is a reason for Hannah's struggle. The enemy is attempting to prevent the conception of the child who will change the fate of all Israel. God had perfect timing for Hannah to conceive, and that moment had not yet arrived.

God looks throughout the earth to find this kind of woman to use in His divine plans. From the beginning of the nation of Israel, the enemy made every effort to prevent a deliverer from arising in Israel.

Hannah's family traveled to Jerusalem each year for the Feast, a time meant for great joy and celebration. However, for Hannah, it became just another opportunity to be publicly tormented by Peninnah, her sister wife. Peninnah continually took pleasure in tormenting Hannah for being barren. In ancient Israel, being unable to have children was considered a disgrace or even a curse.

Peninnah has taken on the role of an adversary. The word "adversary" is pronounced sah-rah' in Hebrew. It signifies tightness and refers to a female rival: adversary, affliction, anguish, distress, tribulation, and trouble. This was the constant reality for Hannah. She lived as the second wife in a household where the first wife had all the children. Hannah was tormented daily by her adversary, the other wife.

When you endure torment, it always originates from a source. This source of torment is darkness, which certainly does not come from God.

Hannah couldn't possibly enjoy this annual festival. She was stuck in a week-long celebration alongside her female rival. Peninnah inflicted suffering, anguish, distress, tribulation, and trouble upon Hannah. How would you react if you were in Hannah's shoes?

You may have experienced something similar. Many of us have endured uncomfortable family reunions or business gatherings with people we'd prefer to avoid. Hannah had to tolerate this all day, every day.

Peninnah viewed Hannah as her rival. That sounds quite familiar. Satan is often called our adversary, which is precisely what the name Satan means—adversary. Where do you think this daily torment began? Hannah's rival was constantly provoking her. What do you think Peninnah's motive or purpose was?

The Hebrew word "provoked" is kaw-as', which means to trouble, grieve, incite rage, stir up anger, experience sorrow, or feel vexed or wroth.

This woman was tormenting Hannah. I wonder how God viewed this whole situation. If Peninnah truly cared for Hannah, she would understand how painful it was for her to endure her barrenness. She would want to offer comfort. A loving response would be to say, "I'm praying for you; I'm hoping for you. You're my friend; you're not my enemy. I'll share my children with you." After all, they were already sharing a husband. At that time, that was the custom.

It's understandable why the Apostle Paul instructed that a bishop should be the husband of one wife. It's evident that having two wives creates significant conflict within a household.

The Hebrew word for fret is raw-am', which means to tumble or be violently agitated. Irritated. Let me ask you this: Does that sound like torment to you?

The definition of torment is:

1. Great physical pain or mental anguish.

2. A source of harassment, annoyance, or pain.

3. The torture inflicted on prisoners under interrogation.

How would it feel to live in a house where you experienced torment every day? Peninnah seemed to take pleasure in watching Hannah become agitated or irritated. To me, there appears to be more than just a spirit of jealousy behind Peninnah's actions. Hannah may have been battling a principality!

There could have even been an angelic struggle in the heavens, similar to what occurred in the book of Daniel. If the enemy is trying to prevent the conception of a deliverer in Israel, he would require more than just a spirit of jealousy to thwart the purposes of God. Hannah was not just praying for her own situation, but for the life and future of a nation! I am sure she did not realize that at the time, but it was already in the making in the spirit realm. God had a plan that would soon be executed to turn the hearts of His people back to Himself! He would use Hannah's son Samuel to do that.

What comes to mind when you hear the word "torment"? "Tormentors"? In the New Testament, Jesus shares a story about being handed over to the tormentors. In Matthew, we learn of a master who is furious with a servant for mistreating another servant; he uses the term tormentors.

> *...his master was wroth with him and turned him over to the tormentors. Matt.18:34*

The term "Tormentor" refers to Satan. "Torment" signifies intense physical suffering or mental anguish, which can sometimes result in physical pain. Additionally, "torment" can imply torture. The disciple John reveals what Satan excels at.

> *,,,,,Satan comes not but to kill, steal and destroy. Jn. 10:10*

He comes to kill your body, steal your finances and peace, and destroy your relationships. That sounds like what Hannah was experiencing. She lost her peace, and now her relationship with her husband is suffering. Hannah is fighting for her peace and mental well-being. She seems to have every reason to feel like she is at war. This is a war of Peninnah's making. Hannah is not the instigator but rather the target of the enemy's aggression and torment.

Hannah began to pray. As she did, she called upon God as "The Lord of Hosts." The Bible doesn't explain why she chose these words. Sometimes, we need to reflect on what we have read and look deeper. It seems she was asking for an army to come and assist her. Was she requesting angelic assistance?

Until this point in scripture, there is no record of this phrase being used to call on God. She is invoking YHVH in a specific manner. "Lord of Hosts" refers to the "God of Angel Armies." Is that what Hannah was requesting to deal with Peninnah's torment?

> *And as he did so year by year, when she went up to the house of the LORD, so she **provoked her;** therefore she wept, and did not eat Then said Elkanah her husband to her, Hannah, why weepest thou? and why eatest thou not? and why is thy **heart grieved**? am not I better to thee than ten sons? 1 Sam. 1:7-8.*

Hannah is so upset and frustrated that she cannot imagine sharing a meal with her family. She's unable to enjoy the festival or take part in the annual offering of sacrifices to God. This has been her reality for years, making it seem relentless. Hannah deeply longed to become a mother and bear a child for Elkanah. Her sadness is intensified by the ongoing torment she endures from Peninnah.

Elkanah understands the reason behind Hannah's distress. He reassures her that he is worth more than ten sons. It's clear why she's in tears. He empathizes with her struggles and recognizes her profound sense of emptiness. He understands her lack of appetite.

> *And she was in bitterness of soul, and **prayed** unto the LORD, and wept sore. And she vowed a vow, and said,* **O LORD of HOST**, *(God of the Armies of Heaven) if thou wilt indeed look on the affliction of thine handmaid, and remember me, and not forget thine handmaid, but wilt give unto thine handmaid a man child, then I will give him unto the LORD all the days of his life, and there shall no razor come upon his head. 1 Sam. 1:10-11.*

In her sorrow, she invoked the God of Heaven's Armies.

The name of God in Hebrew is *YHVH;* it means self-existent or eternal. It's the Hebrew national name of God. Since there are no vowels in the Hebrew language, no one is entirely sure how the Holy Name of God is pronounced.

Host: This word in Hebrew refers to a large group of people, especially one that is systematically organized for warfare (an army). This term suggests a campaign, battle, company, or group of soldiers who are ready for war.

Hannah did not address Him as the Lord of Mercy, God the Healer, or Provider. Rather, she referred to Him as the Lord of Hosts, the God of Armies—those assembled for combat. She was summoning The General, expressing a genuine need for substantial help. She called upon the Hosts, the soldiers armed for conflict. So, who makes up that army? God commands an angelic host, warriors equipped for battle combat.

Could there be another explanation for why Hannah hadn't conceived? Would a woman easily relinquish her only child to be raised by a priest rather than in her own home? Would Hannah have consented to such an arrangement if she hadn't fought against the curse of infertility for so long? It all revolves around God's timing and the purpose He has for everyone affected, including the nation of Israel as a whole.

I want to remind you that the angels are here to serve those who inherit salvation; that's us. They are also present and prepared to help us with our personal struggles. While we might not see the angels, they can see us clearly. Once we fully embrace God's Kingdom, we will receive our glorified bodies, and our spiritual sight will be awakened. On that day, we'll easily recognize one another.

Secret: Angels Rescue in Personal Conflicts

It seems that Hannah understands spiritual warfare. Does she also acknowledge the help of angels? Does she remember that Sarah conceived after the angels appeared before the destruction of Sodom and Gomorrah?

Remember that Abraham and Sarah longed for a child. They desired it so intensely that they took matters into their own hands at one point and ended up with Ishmael. Sometimes, we lack the faith to wait on God or trust His plan, leading us to pursue our own paths. Never forget that your ideas and plans cannot compare to God's plans for you. He promises to bless us and to provide us with a hope and a future.

> *For I know the plans I have for you," declares the Lord, "plans to prosper you and not to harm you, plans to give you hope and a future. Jer. 29:11*

I want to illustrate a connection here, so we'll briefly examine the story of Sarah and the angels. Abraham was resting under the Mamre tree when three men appeared to him. These men turned out to be angels. One of them appeared to be God Himself in human form. As mentioned in Chapter Four, the Hebrew people believed in two aspects of the same God: one who was invisible and another who manifested in the flesh.

Secret: Sometimes Angels Come Looking for You.

You'll be amazed at how often God reveals Himself in a visible form. We connect with Him more easily when He appears to us in that way (i.e., Jesus). I believe this paves the way for the entire house of Israel to embrace Jesus/Yeshua. He is the God who manifested in the flesh and paid our debt at Calvary.

When the angels appear, they seem to be looking for Sarah.

> *Then they said to him, "Where is Sarah your wife?" And he said, "There, in the tent." He said, "I will surely return to you at this time next year; and behold,* ***Sarah your wife will have a son.****" And Sarah was listening at the tent door, which was behind him. Now Abraham and Sarah* ***were old,*** *well advanced in years; she was past [the age of] childbearing. So Sarah laughed to herself [when she heard the LORD'S words], saying, "After I have become old, shall I have pleasure and delight, my lord (husband) being also old?" And the LORD asked Abraham, "Why did Sarah laugh [to herself], saying, 'Shall I really give birth [to a child] when I am so old?'* ***Is anything too difficult*** *or too wonderful for the LORD? At the appointed time, when the season [for her delivery] comes,* ***I will return*** *to you and Sarah will have a son." Gen. 18:9-14 Amp.*

Imagine this for a moment: what if you were in her shoes? How would you feel? She has dreamed of having a child for as long as she can remember. After facing so many heartaches, it's hard to keep track of them all. And now, it seems like time has slipped away from her. What emotions would you experience in that situation?

In the natural, Sarah's body could not produce an egg to be fertilized, making conception virtually impossible. While she believed she could no longer have a child, nothing is impossible with God.

I am sure that by this time, Sarah had resolved to die childless. One of the angels reminds her, "Is anything too difficult for God?" We need to ask ourselves that every day. The answer is no. Nothing, nothing is too difficult for God.

We know what happened. After the angels departed, Sarah conceived, and the promised son, Isaac, was born. It took a visit from an angel before Sarah could conceive. The Apocrypha tells us that the angels that visited Sarah, healed her womb. Now, let's examine the phrase "Lord of Hosts." again.:

The literal meaning in Hebrew is "**Lord of Armies**". Tza-va (צבא) is the word for army – and what today refers to the Israeli Defense Force. Tza-va-ot (צבאות) is the plural, multiple armies.

Is it inherently a military term? What does it signify for us when we refer to God as the "Lord of Armies"?

Armies: A large, organized group of armed personnel trained for war. We know there are other types of angels. However, do you remember the worshiping angels in Chapter One? They were first seen worshiping God, but when the devil appeared, they began to fight. I suspect that every angel is trained for battle. If there's a call to duty, they respond.

Not long ago, an angel appeared during our group prayer time to help us pray. I have seen many angels, but this was the first time one spoke to me. I asked him why he had come, and he answered my question. Remember, I told you to ask more questions, and you will receive more answers. He wasn't a warring angel; even though he had a weapon at his side, he was here to fulfill a different assignment. He never drew his weapon because his purpose was to support us.

It was a cold, rainy night, and we didn't expect anyone to show up for prayer. We could have easily canceled, but Ben and I decided to pray, even if it was just the two of us. I tidied up the house, set up the whiteboard to note prayer requests, and started the worship music. We were pleasantly surprised when a sister in a wheelchair arrived to join us in prayer. As we sought God, the Spirit of the Lord descended. She said, "I feel like a portal has just opened in the heavens." Then I heard the Lord say, "Open your eyes." When I did, I saw a huge angel. I told the others, "We have a visitor." The ceiling in our living room is vaulted; this angel stood in front of the fireplace and filled the entire room from floor to ceiling. He was enormous.

I closed my eyes again. When I opened them, he had changed positions. He had become smaller in size, more like a tall man. He was kneeling on one knee on the floor right next to me. He wore sandals and a knee-length white garment. His belt held a sheath with a sword inside. He bowed his head as if he were praying with us.

I asked, "Why have you come?" He replied, "I have come to help you pray. God is honoring your loyalty and commitment to your word." We had agreed as a group to pray each Monday night. When others didn't join us, the angel was assigned to assist us. The three of us had an incredible night of prayer, basking in the presence of the Father.

Other angels are assigned to protect us. So, when we see angels in a ring of fire around our property, we know they are here for our defense. If they needed to fight, I'm confident they would mobilize immediately. They are here to assist us with any needs we have.

They may appear when you pray, just like they did with Daniel. You may not see them, but they are present regardless.

Some translations interpret Yahweh Sabaoth as "Lord of the Angel Armies." So how will the General of this vast army respond to Hannah's request?

Eli, the priest, saw her praying silently. He saw her mouth move, but he couldn't hear her speak. When he accused her of being drunk, she responded in this manner:

> *Count not thine handmaid for a daughter of Belial: for out of the abundance of my complaint and **grief** have I spoken hitherto. Then Eli answered and said, Go in peace: and the God of Israel **grant thee thy petition** that thou hast asked of him And she said, Let thine handmaid find grace in thy sight. So the woman went her way, and did eat, and her countenance was no more sad. 1 Sam. 1:16-18*

Hannah told Eli, "I am not a child of the devil. I am a child of God." She didn't even share with Eli what she was praying for; he agreed with whatever her petition was. So, there is the Biblical principle again: in the voice of two or three witnesses, let every word be established.

The High Priest set himself in agreement with Hannah's plea. The Word tells us that where any two of you are gathered together to pray and are in agreement, God is in the midst of you. Eli had blessed her and declared, "May the God of Heaven grant your petition."

> *And they rose up in the morning early, and worshipped before the Lord, and returned, and came to their house to Ramah: and Elkanah knew Hannah his wife; and the Lord remembered her. Wherefore it came to pass, when the time was come about after Hannah had conceived, that she bare a son, and called his name Samuel, saying, Because I have asked him of the Lord. 1 Sam. 1:19-20*

Secret: What seems like a personal battle may be much more important than you imagine. Your victory might change the course of a nation.

Hannah prayed through. Her prayer changed her entire mindset. She was able to move forward in faith, and through prayer, she overcame her sadness. It's true that she still had an adversary, but God would deal with that too.

When we pray through, we pray until we make a connection with God. Once we have done that, we know He has heard our petitions. We can walk away with the assurance that we have received what we have asked of Him.

> *And this is the confidence that we have in him, that, if we ask anything according to his will, he heareth us: And if we know that he hear us, whatsoever we ask, we know that we have the petitions that we desired of him. 1 Jn. 5:14-15*

When I was young in the Lord, it was not unusual to see people go to the altar and pray for hours. Sometimes, they would pray all night long. That kind of prayer has faded away. We don't see that anymore. In fact, in many churches, there is no altar to visit. Instead, there is a back room for those who wish to pray. As a result, the congregation doesn't witness people praying through to victory. We don't ever realize that they have clung to God until their assurance came. It has all been relegated to the back room.

Hannah remained in the presence of God until she felt assured that He had heard her prayers; she was confident.

When you rise from prayer, knowing that God has heard, you feel a sense of satisfaction. You trust that the answer is on its way. God will communicate with your heart, too, and reassure you that He has your situation under control.

If you haven't read my book "Letting Them Go, Trusting God to Catch Them," you don't know that I had a daughter who was missing for fifteen years. I didn't know whether she was dead or alive.

At first, I behaved like Hannah; I prayed endlessly, cried, and found myself on the floor, exhausted, pleading with God for her return. My daughter was like my best friend. She and I had prayed together countless times and experienced significant spiritual breakthroughs. The conflict came when she married someone who essentially removed her from our lives.

I didn't know where she was or how she was doing. I had grandchildren I didn't even know about. But when I fully surrendered to God's will, the Holy Spirit spoke to me, saying, "Get up, stop crying, and move on with your life. She'll return, but it will happen in my time, not yours."

That was a hard word to hear, but once I did, I was able to move forward with my life. I was in nursing school at that time. With God's reassurance of her return, I could concentrate and graduate at the top of my class from a major university. Until then, I had been completely distracted by the loss of my daughter. If I hadn't heard from God, I wouldn't have succeeded in what He had called me to during that time in my life.

Believers don't know how to pray through anymore; we need God to teach us. We must revive that lost art of staying in God's presence until we receive an answer. Hannah had an advantage that others didn't. She understood there was a "God of Armies" and that if she needed an army, God would send an army to rescue her. She knew He would do it.

Why is Samuel's birth so significant? Why would the enemy try so hard to prevent Hannah from conceiving? This child, Samuel, was a deliverer sent by God. He would change the course of the nation of Israel. He was the first of the prophets. It's said that he served as the bridge between Moses and the prophets Elijah and Elisha.

In a way, this story reminds me of the scripture in Revelations:

> ……: *and the dragon stood before the woman which was ready to be delivered, for to devour her child as soon as it was born. Rev. 12:4b*

Could it be that this is the enemy's intention in the story as well? Is the devil doing everything he can to stop the birth of a true man of God who will serve as a deliverer in Israel?

After Hannah's struggles in prayer with God, He blessed her with a son, whom she named Samuel. She dedicated him and consecrated him to God. I believe she and the angel armies broke through and healed Hannah's womb just as the angels did for Sarah. In a sense, Hannah wrestled with an angel, much like Jacob did.

At the time that Hannah took Samuel to Shiloh, Israel was oppressed by the Philistines. Idolatry was widespread across the land, and the office of the High Priest Eli was deeply corrupt. Eli and both of his sons died the day the Ark of the Covenant was captured by the Philistines, which was devastating for the Hebrews. The presence of God, the Ark of the Covenant, had fallen into enemy hands,

The task of leading the nation was then passed to Samuel. In one day, the responsibility of a nation fell on this young man. He would do it God's way or not at all.

God worked through the great judge and prophet Samuel to guide Israel, who had strayed, back to a path of repentance. He helped them celebrate their very first Passover correctly since the days of Joshua! Even as a boy, Samuel was attuned to hearing God's voice when no one else did. Psalm 99 places Samuel alongside Moses and Aaron. His leadership is compared to that of Moses. He led Israel's army to triumph over their constant enemies.

Hannah expressed a prayer of gratitude, located in First Samuel 2. It serves as a magnificent tribute to the "Lord of Hosts." In one part of that prayer, Hannah proclaims:

> *"It is not by strength that one prevails; those who oppose the Lord will be broken. The Most High will **thunder** from heaven; the Lord will judge the ends of the earth. 1 Sam.2:10*

This is the power of Hannah's prayer for her son. Israel was being pursued by the Philistines and was in great fear until God **thundered** and turned the battle around.

> *And as Samuel was offering up the burnt offering, the Philistines drew near to battle against Israel: but **the Lord thundered** with a **great thunder** on that day upon the Philistines and discomfited them; and they were smitten before Israel. 1 Sam 7:10*

Hannah was an extraordinary woman; even in her prayers, she expressed prophetic wisdom to rescue her son and all of Israel from their adversary. Hannah had prayed for her son as a child that God would thunder from heaven. As a man, Samuel led the armies of Israel in war, and God did just as Hannah had prayed. He thundered from heaven to defeat Israel's enemies and fulfilled the prayer of a mother praying for her young son. What an amazing God we serve!

How many of your prayers are stored up for the future like Hannah's were?

Samuel, who is esteemed for his wisdom and spiritual insight, anointed both King Saul and King David. He consistently advised King David and aided in outlining the components needed for the Temple that David wished to construct. He established the first school of the Prophets. He was recognized as a distinguished writer and historian, and he is included in the "Hall of Faith" found in the Book of Hebrews. While the people of his time were consumed by their own selfishness, Samuel set himself apart as a man of honor.

> *"And what shall I more say? for the time would fail me to tell of Gedeon, and of Barak, and of Samson, and of Jephthae; of David also, and Samuel, and of the prophets:" Heb. 11:32*

Hannah's battle was more than a struggle with barrenness and an earthly adversary. Her struggle was to birth a ***deliverer*** and to change the course of a nation headed the wrong way. The vindication of God is perfect in this story. Peninnah had children, but Hannah gave birth to the first prophet of Israel.

Secret: *When the devil attacks you by using another person, YOU may request Angel Armies to assist you in your personal battles.*

This exemplifies a form of spiritual warfare that we frequently miss while studying the Word. Hannah triumphed over her foe by appealing to the "God of Angel Armies." Notably, among all instances of the phrase "Lord of Host" or "God of Angel Armies," Hannah was the first to invoke this title.

Consider the emotions and suffering that Hannah endured. Who do you believe was behind the harassment? While it may have appeared to come from a person, it was instigated by the one who comes to kill, steal, and destroy. Demonic forces are behind torment, and that's what Hannah was fighting against. She dealt with constant agitation and faced a daily struggle. This battle was fought through **words**, innuendos, and actions.

Never forget that God sees and cares. If He needs to send an **entire army** to rescue you from your tormentors, He will do it! We can be certain the angels know exactly what's behind every attack the enemy sends your way.

Secret: *God Doesn't just Win Battles. He Takes Back What the Devil Stole.*

This is just part of Hannah's prayer for Thanksgiving.

> *For this child I prayed; and the LORD hath given me my petition which I asked of him: Therefore also I have lent him to the LORD; as long as he liveth he shall be lent to the LORD. And she worshipped the LORD there. 1 Sam. 1:26-28*

> *And Hannah prayed, and said, My heart rejoiceth in the LORD, mine horn is exalted in the LORD: **my mouth is enlarged over mine enemies**; because I rejoice in thy salvation. There is none*

> *holy as the LORD: for there is none beside thee: neither is there any rock like our God. Talk no more so exceeding proudly; let not arrogancy come out of your mouth: for the LORD is a God of knowledge, and by him actions are weighed. The bows of the mighty men are broken, and they that stumbled are girded with strength. 1 Sam. 2:1-4*

Do you believe Hannah felt vindicated? This prayer says it all. She calls it like it is. She says that she triumphed over her enemies. She rebukes that enemy by saying "Stop talking so proudly and let not arrogance come out of your mouth." Who do you think she is talking about? Peninnah?

> *And Eli blessed Elkanah and his wife, and said, The LORD give thee seed of this woman for the loan which is lent to the LORD. And they went unto their own home. And the LORD visited Hannah, so that she conceived, and bare **three sons and two daughters**. And the child Samuel grew before the LORD. 2 Sam. 20-21*

Hannah gave birth to three additional sons and two daughters.

> *And Samuel grew, and the LORD was with him, and did let none of his words fall to the ground. And all Israel from Dan even to Beersheba knew that **Samuel was established to be a prophet of the Lord**. 1 Sam. 3:19-20*

Hallelujah! I am so amazed at the wonder of our King.

We often overlook the fact that angels have been watching over us since birth. They are perpetually on duty, accompanying us wherever we venture. Find comfort in this truth; you don't have to wait for their presence—they are there with you the moment you call out to God.

Chapter 7

Angels to the Rescue!

Let's take a closer look at a couple of God's champions in some of the most beloved stories found in the scriptures. There are countless wonderful tales that highlight angelic interventions, but this one stands out for its clarity. You may find that there are some delightful details you overlooked that are worth exploring further.

Let's begin with the inspiring prophet Elisha! He had the privilege of being mentored by the esteemed prophet Elijah, who ascended to heaven in a glorious chariot of fire. Elisha displayed unwavering loyalty and courage, standing faithfully by Elijah's side as he embraced God's will. His extraordinary journey is illustrated in the captivating accounts in 1 Kings and 2 Kings, which highlight his remarkable miracles and profound commitment to God's purpose.

Elijah was aware of God's plan to take him to heaven without dying. He would be taken up in a chariot of fire. His plan was to be alone for this momentous and miraculous event. So he tried unsuccessfully to convince Elisha to leave his side. Yet, Elisha remained determined, believing that accompanying Elijah during his ascent would enable him to inherit a double portion of Elijah's prophetic mantle. With resolute determination, he expressed his steadfast commitment, saying, "As surely as the LORD lives and you live, I will not leave you."

His extraordinary loyalty paid off. When Elijah ascended to heaven, Elisha was there to witness this spectacular event. As Elijah went up, his mantle fell on Elisha. He received a double portion of Elijah's anointing, allowing him to operate with twice the power of his predecessor. It was immediately evident that Elijah's miraculous ministry had passed to Elisha.

> *Then it happened, as they continued on and talked, that suddenly a chariot of fire appeared with horses of fire and separated the two of them; and Elijah went up by a whirlwind into heaven. And Elisha saw it, and he cried out, "My father, my father, the chariot of Israel and its horsemen!" So he saw him no more. And he took hold of his own clothes and tore them into two pieces. He also took up the mantle of Elijah that had fallen from him and went back and stood by the bank of the Jordan. Then he took the mantle of Elijah that had fallen from him, and struck the water, and said, "Where is the Lord God of Elijah?" And when he also had struck the water, it was divided this way and that; and Elisha crossed over. 2 Kings. 2:11-14*

Holy smokes! What an awesome, glorious experience! What kind of lasting impression do you think it left on Elisha? No wonder he was fearless!

Elisha operated with the understanding that he had angelic assistance working with him. We resume this part of the story in 1 Kings 6. The Syrian army was struggling in its military campaigns against Israel. Their king began to suspect he had a spy in his ranks who was feeding Israel information about their planned attacks. Upon investigation, he discovered that Israel's greatest asset was the prophet, Elisha. Elisha was receiving divine revelations concerning the strategies of the Syrian army and had been advising Israel on how to evade every enemy plan. No matter how strong the Syrian intelligence was, it could not surpass the knowledge that God imparted to Elisha.

This scripture passage beautifully illustrates the "unseen realm." It clearly shows that on one hill, there is the vast visible Syrian army, and on another, there is an even greater invisible angelic army.

The King of Syria realized that his spy was Elisha, and he aimed to capture him. He planned to bring him back to Syria, so he sent an entire army to surround Elisha's home solely to capture him. Just think about it—an entire army is mobilized to capture just one man!

Early that morning, Elisha's servant stepped outside. He hurried back in, overwhelmed with fear at the sight of the enemy surrounding them. However, Elisha remained calm and composed. To reassure his servant, he prayed for him to see the spiritual realm as Elisha did.

What Elisha understood was that God's unseen warriors were there to protect him. God didn't need to dispatch these angels or create them when they were necessary. They were already present and ready for battle. Your angels are with you. They don't need to be summoned. They stand ready to act the moment you call upon the Lord.

I understand that it can be challenging to grasp. However, what's documented in the scriptures is that Elisha didn't pray for the angels to come; he was confident they were already there. He only wanted his servant to be able to see them. Protection from an armed army of warring angels was already present. How did the angels know to be there at the same time the Syrians showed up?

> *The eyes of the Lord are everywhere, keeping watch on the wicked and the good. Pr. 15:3*

God sees everything. Those who engage in dark deeds behind closed doors may be hiding from others, but nothing is hidden from Him. The angels were always working with Elisha; this was nothing new to him. It was what he expected.

Secret: Get it in your spirit that God sees and knows everything. Nothing escapes Him!

Every time I get into my car, I thank God for the angels assigned to me. I know they are traveling with me. I have witnessed incredible and unexplainable events during my travels that can only be attributed to angelic intervention. I know they are there.

The servant focused on the vast Syrian army directly in front of him—what he could perceive with his physical eyes in the natural world. That's a natural response. We often feel so confident in our understanding of what we have seen in the natural world that we immediately devise our own plans of action. Most believers have never attempted to cultivate their spiritual eyes to see. The supernatural frightens them.

There is nothing mystical about seeing or hearing in the Spirit. When we are born again, we become part of the kingdom of God, which is not of this world. We are told that we are seated in heavenly places with Christ Jesus. If He sees, then why would it be strange or unusual for a child of God to see and hear in the Spirit? You are one with Him.

> *The natural person does not accept the **things of the Spirit** of God, for they are folly to him, and he is not able to understand them because they are **spiritually discerned**. 1 Cor. 2:14*

The things of God are spiritually discerned. For a person to see in the spirit requires spiritual eyes. That's why Elisha could see an angelic army while the servant could not. Don't find it strange when others perceive things you don't. One day, the situation may be reversed, and you will see what others cannot. Be careful not to judge.

> *He has blinded their eyes and hardened their heart, lest they **see** with their eyes, and **understand** with their heart, and turn, and I would heal them." Isaiah said these things because he saw his glory and spoke of him. Jn. 12:41*

> *And [I pray] that the eyes of your heart [the very center and core of your being] may be enlightened [flooded with light by the Holy Spirit], so that you will know and cherish the hope [the divine guarantee, the confident expectation] to which He has called you,*

> *the riches of His glorious inheritance in the saints (God's people), Eph. 1:18 Amp.*

Our spiritual understanding truly blossoms from our hearts. While we all view the world with our physical eyes, the eyes Jesus speaks of in the scripture above refer to those deep within our hearts (or spirits). Paul shares that if we can embrace the vision of our hearts, we will uncover the incredible riches of His glory. Just imagine experiencing a whole hill filled with angelic warriors in chariots of fire—that's a beautiful glimpse of God's glory!

Notice in the following scriptures how frequently these verses refer to the eyes in relation to bringing about God's glory and deliverance. First, Elisha prays for his servant to have his eyes opened, even though he already sees with his natural vision. Then, he prays for the enemy's eyes to be blinded, even though they can still see with their physical sight. Finally, he prays for the enemy to regain their sight, for their eyes to be opened again.

> *When the servant of the man of God got up and went out early the next morning, an army with horses and chariots had surrounded the city. Oh no, my lord! What shall we do?" the servant asked.* ***"Don't be afraid,"*** *the prophet answered.* ***"Those who are with us are more*** *than those who are with them. 2 Kings 6:15-16*

Regardless of how large the enemy's army may be, God always has one that is even larger. Our God can surpass Satan at every turn. He is the creator of all things. There are no surprises for God. Everything the devil does is merely a copy of what he observes God doing. He can only imitate.

Secret: Pay attention: The supernatural of Satan is a copy of Our God. Nothing is original to him.

Elisha said to his servant, "Don't be afraid." Although Elisha could already see the angelic army, he wanted his servant to see it, too. So, he prayed for his servant.

The angelic army had chariots of fire, while the enemy had no such weaponry. Imagine the awe that swept over the servant as he witnessed the chariots of fire!

> *For our God is a consuming fire. Heb. 12:29*

Secret: Did you know blinding the enemy is one of the angel's weapons?

In the coming days, if you ever need to hide in plain sight, follow Elisha's example: ask the angels to bring blindness to the enemy's camp.

> *"And Elisha prayed, "**Open** his eyes, LORD, so that he may see." Then the LORD opened the servant's eyes, and he looked and saw the hills full of horses and **chariots of fire** all around Elisha. As the enemy came down toward him, Elisha prayed to the LORD, "Strike this army with **blindness**." So he struck them with blindness, as Elisha had asked. Elisha told them, "This is not the road and this is not the city. Follow me, and I will lead you to the man you are looking for." And he led them to Samaria. After they entered the city, Elisha said, "LORD, open the eyes of these men so they can see." Then the LORD opened their eyes and they looked, and there they were, inside Samaria. 2 Kings 6:17-20*

They were led deep into enemy territory. Ask yourself, who do you think blinded the enemy's eyes? In the story of Sodom and Gomorrah, it was the angels who struck the aggressors with blindness. I'm guessing the angels are at work here as well. What do you think? Blindness is one of the angels' weapons.

Secret: A strategic weapon in warfare may require a lie!

The enemy lies daily; if they're speaking, they're likely deceiving. At most, it's a half-truth.

Elisha told the Syrians they were wrong about their location. He misled them by claiming they had the wrong person and were in the wrong city. They believed him. Consequently, Elisha intentionally led them into the camp of their enemies. It's crucial for us to listen to the Lord's voice. When He reveals a plan or strategy, follow His guidance quickly and without hesitation, even if it feels out of character. It could save your life.

Were the Syrian soldiers blind to everything? Were they literally stumbling in the dark? Or were they just selectively blind, unable to recognize Elisha or realize where they were being led? Think about it. Elisha truly was hiding in plain sight.

Did the angel army go with Elisha as he led the Syrians to Samaria? The scripture doesn't tell us. What do you think?

This passage underscores several crucial points. A major one is the extensive resources at God's disposal. The key verse declares, "Those who are with us are MORE than those who are with them." This will FOREVER be true in our spiritual battles; there will always be greater forces on our side than against us if we remain in covenant with Yeshua/Jesus.

In this intriguing moment, we see the contrast between sight and blindness, faith and doubt. Elisha possessed a deep knowledge that extended beyond what the human eyes could perceive, while his servant struggled with doubt and sought tangible proof. To him, it seemed the Syrian army held the upper hand; however, the will of the enemy soldiers was overridden by the will of God. The very cells in their bodies responded to their Creator's command, leading to a sudden loss of their God-given ability to see.

This is what Jesus said about our need to see with spiritual eyes:

> *"If you love me, you will keep my commands; and I will ask the Father, and he will give you another comforting Counselor like me, the Spirit of Truth, to be with you forever. The world cannot receive him, because it neither **sees** nor knows him. You know him, because he is staying with you and will be united with you. I will not leave you orphans—I am coming to you. In just a little*

while, ***the world will no longer see me;*** *but* ***you will see me.*** *Because I live, you too will live. Jn. 14:15-19*

Jesus is physically leaving the earth, but he tells his disciples that they will still **see** him. How are they able to see someone who is no longer living on this earth? They are able to **see** him through the power of the Holy Spirit that will live in them. He expects them to have spiritual eyes to see him, even after his ascension.

When Elisha brought the Syrian army into their enemy's territory, the King of Israel saw them and said to Elisha:

My father, shall I smite them? shall I smite them? And he answered, Thou shalt not smite them: wouldest thou smite those whom thou hast taken captive with thy sword and with thy bow? set bread and water before them, that they may eat and drink, and go to their master. And he prepared great provision for them: and when they had eaten and drunk, he sent them away, and they went to their master. So, the bands of Syria came no more into the land of Israel. 2 Kings 6: 21-23

Elisha's response illustrates the essence of true strength and what it truly means to achieve victory. In contrast, the King of Israel's reaction seems almost comical. He asked Elisha, "Can I kill them? Can I kill them? Can I? Can I? Huh?" The answer was "No." Instead, they prepared a grand feast for their captives and sent them on their way. Subsequently, the fighting ceased—the Syrians simply stopped coming. They had been treated kindly by their enemies.

This may have been the very first time the Syrians experienced kind treatment from what they viewed as an adversary.

There is so much hate in our world; people are taught to hate others from birth. Sometimes, there's an inexplicable aversion towards a person or even a whole group of people. Frequently, the root of this feeling lies in our lack of understanding about them. We think we know them and feel justified in our opinions. However, when we find ourselves facing a challenge together and are forced to support one another, that's when we start to uncover who they really are. We often realize that we have misunderstood them without even knowing it.

So, let me ask you directly: what do you think? Do you believe that God suddenly created that army for Elisha, or do you think that army was always there? If it was always there, what are the implications for you and me?

I believe the answer is that God has always had an army. When Elisha stepped out of his house to see the enemy, he wasn't shaking. He simply asked God to open his servant's eyes. It was no big deal for Elisha. God's army was already present. Elisha was accustomed to having angelic assistance available in times of danger. The servant had never seen anything like chariots of fire, and neither have most of us. That's why I wrote this book. We need to understand that God's protection takes many forms, and angel armies are just one of them.

We need to recognize that the armies are present even if we don't see them. Elisha could see angels when others could not. This serves as a reminder that we may not always perceive what others can clearly see.

We learned in previous chapters that the Angels are our fellow servants. They are here to minister for (not to) those who shall be heirs of salvation.

> *But to which of the angels said he at any time, Sit on my right hand, until I make thine enemies thy footstool? Are they not all ministering spirits, sent forth to minister for them who shall be heirs of salvation? Heb.1:14*

Let's remember that we are beloved children of the Most High God. He has lovingly made provisions for us, His special family. He created us and the angels, too. We exist in this earthly realm, and while we may not always see our heavenly family, they are always close by. They are amazing allies in our spiritual journey, even if we might not always recognize it. Always remember: YOU are never truly alone!

We learned earlier that the angels came for Daniel's words. We witnessed their presence during our local group prayer times. They come because of the powerful words of truth being declared as the saints pray and worship. Your words are immensely powerful weapons!

Yeshua is The Word. He has been here since the beginning. He spoke everything into existence, and when He returns, He will defeat the enemy with the words of His mouth!

We are made in His image. We are the only species on Earth that has the ability to use words, and yet we don't. Do we think that when we are faced with the unthinkable, we will suddenly begin to use our words? Now is the time to exercise our senses to discern good from evil and to start doing as our great teacher, Yeshua, did. Use our words to wage war. Take the authority and dominion that has been given to you as humankind!

We are followers of Yeshua. As we observe Him, we transform into His likeness. He stated that His purpose was to eradicate the devil's works. We reflect Him and are called to emulate what we have witnessed Him doing.

> *"He that committeth sin is of the devil; for the devil sinneth from the beginning. For this purpose the Son of God was manifested, that* **He might destroy the works of the devil.***"* 1 Jn. 3;8

That's why Jesus came. Satan upset the apple cart in Eden. He took authority that he didn't possess, and he has been attempting to do that ever since. Yeshua came to eliminate his works; to put an end to the devastation he has inflicted upon this earth. That's why YOU are part of His army. You are meant to be dismantling the works of the devil!

The way you do that is in prayer, the way you pray is with words, and words are weapons.

The way Yeshua overcomes is by the breath of His mouth. He spoke the earth into existence, and he will slay the enemy with his Words.

> *Then the lawless one [the Antichrist] will be revealed and the Lord Jesus will **slay him with the breath of His mouth** and bring him to an end by the appearance of His coming. 2 Th. 2:8*

> *But with righteousness and justice He will judge the poor, And decide with fairness for the downtrodden of the earth; And He shall strike the earth with the rod of His mouth, And with the **breath of His lips** He shall slay the wicked. Isa. 11:4*

The word "rod" in Hebrew refers to a stick used for punishment, fighting, ruling, or correction. That's the purpose of the rod.

Of his mouth: p*eh in the Hebrew and it means* the *mouth* (**particularly speech**) a **sentence**, to talk.

That is how Yeshua/Jesus confronts His enemies: with His words. You are made in His image, and you, too, combat with words.

Elisha wasn't the only one who knew he had warring angels to fight for him. So did David!

David's warfare prayer:

> *A Psalm of David. Plead my cause, O LORD, with them that strive with me: fight against them that fight against me. Ps. 35:1*

He is requesting God to defend him. Have you ever felt as though someone or something is opposing you? Do you ever sense another is struggling with you? Are you facing false accusations like David did? He sought God's intervention to advocate for him and battle on his behalf.

> *Take hold of shield and buckler, and stand up for mine help. Draw out also the spear, and stop the way against them that persecute me: say unto my soul, I am thy salvation. Ps. 35:2-3*

It seems David is asking God to strengthen his faith so that he can trust in God as his help and salvation. We may encounter times of persecution. This is how we are to pray.

He asks God to speak to his soul. He wants to hear God say, "I AM. I AM, I AM your salvation. Nothing else will save you except I AM."

> *Let them be confounded and put to shame that seek after my soul: let them be turned back and brought to confusion that devise my hurt. Ps. 35:4*

I believe this serves as a compelling example of how we should pray against the forces of darkness that may be opposing us. These individuals are actively seeking David's very soul. That's the devil's plan for you, your children, and the ones you love. He seeks their souls.

Now, I want you to understand David's request: Send the Angel of the Lord to pursue them, to persecute them.

> *Let them be as chaff before the wind: and let the **angel** of the LORD **chase them**. Ps. 35:5*

Secret: You can ask for angels to chase the enemy and to persecute them.

Angels drive evil away, just as my young children witnessed in the church. They beheld a battle between good and evil. The Angels of God chased the evil angels and ran them out of the sanctuary! Then, it says in verse 6:

> *Let their way be dark and slippery: and let the **angel** of the LORD **persecute** them. Ps. 35:6*

David is asking for the angel of the Lord to persecute his enemies. I heard a minister say this week that we shouldn't pray this way. Someone should have informed David about that. We are also cautioned against seeking a sign. We are not looking for a sign. The angels are already present with us. We are doing the same thing David did in this scripture. He is asking

God to send help that he can't even see, but he will see the results of his request. We can't cause an angel to manifest; that is part of God's sovereignty. We just keep worshiping God, and they keep doing what they are called to do as fellow servants.

Individuals who comprehend the supernatural realm understand that we don't have to navigate this alone. We have support. The battle is the Lord's!

The phrase "Let their way be dark" includes misery. destruction, death, and sorrow.

The word slippery means a treacherous spot.

The word chase is **to *run after*** (**usually with hostile intent**; to chase, put to flight, follow after, **hunt,** and **pursue**

David is bold in his prayers. He is specific about the help he seeks from his unseen family. Due to the actions of David's enemies, he requests the angels to repay them in kind. They have set a trap for David without cause, so he asks God to make them fall into their own trap.

> *For without cause they hid their net for me; Without cause they dug a pit [of destruction] for my life. Ps. 35:7 Amp.*

In summary of our journey so far, Hannah reached out to Yahweh, the Lord of Hosts and the Lord of Angel Armies, with a heartfelt prayer to overcome her adversary and bless her with a son. She poured her emotions into her prayers, a practice some lovingly call praying through, until she felt a sense of peace wash over her. The weight on her heart started to lift as she found comfort in the assurance that God had listened to her heartfelt plea. Her confidence blossomed, knowing that He would respond in His perfect way.

When you pray, don't lose heart while waiting for your answer. You may be tempted to lay your burden down on the altar only to pick it back up again. Then, you keep trying to figure out how to fix things on your own.

How exhausting! God's ways are higher than our ways, and His answers are better.

Hannah was certainly aware that Sarah conceived after the angel visited her. She had prayed and poured her heart out for a child many times, but it was granted after the angels visited her. We are told in the Book of Jasher that when the angels visited Sarah, they healed her and opened her womb. She was 90 years old. I wonder how many tears Sarah shed over being barren.

How many tears have you shed? What are you trusting God for?

Secret: Angels bring healing.

This was a miraculous birth in God's perfect timing, and we see the answer to Sarah's prayer come with an angelic visit. Despite all the conflict that Sarah had with Hagar and Ishmael, I'm quite sure that Sarah felt her prayers were a form of warfare. She experienced the same torment that Hannah endured, but hers came from Hagar.

Now we have the story of Elijah: He prayed for the servant's eyes to be opened to see what was already there. What a sight! Elisha prayed for the army to become blind, and it happened. Angels were there to protect Elisah. They showed up when he needed them. He didn't even know he was surrounded by enemies, and God had already sent an army of angels to protect him.

The Word tells us that sometimes we entertain angels unaware. What is around us that we don't see?

Lastly, we reflected on David's prayer to confront his enemies. He was tormented and fighting for his life when he called for the Angel of God. We don't pray to angels; they are our fellow servants. However, we seek their assistance in warfare, and that's what this entire book is about: angelic assistance in battle. Hopefully, you are learning to engage in Spiritual Warfare and that your prayers are not merely a wish list for God.

If Jesus came to destroy the works of the devil, and we are to follow his example, we better get busy. There's a lot to fight for; we want to see the Kingdom of God come to this earth. Your words have the right, the ability, the dominion, and the power to work with Jesus in destroying the works of the devil.

Our local prayer team has been blessed to witness angel armies on this property. That was amazing because two of us saw the same thing at the same time. It doesn't always happen that way, so when it does, it removes all doubt. You don't second-guess yourself or wonder, "Did I really see all that?"

An entire army stood on the back ridge of the property. All were on horseback and armed. Everything was white. The soldiers wore white, the weapons gleamed white, and the horses shone white. None of these angels had wings, but the horses did. I thought, Wow! No wonder it's such a swift army; the horses have wings. They were staggered in formation so that none of the horses' wings touched each other. They looked as if they were awaiting orders to charge.

The world has jets, drones, and modern equipment that the enemy has helped them to invent for evil. The devil has assisted the world in developing its murderous weapons of mass destruction and war. But don't for a second believe that every weapon of war that mankind or the enemy possesses is something God can't surpass. He has many more and far greater weapons than the enemy.

God has two families, and they are here to assist one another. That's what we, as overcomers and the angels, do for the Kingdom of God on this earth.

We have been taught about the armor of God. We know about the sword of the spirit, which is the Word of God. Now you know that we can learn to pray like David. Praying The Word of God assures us that our words never return void. When they come back, they will have produced what God intended for them to.

We continue to wear the entire Armor of God. We have our loins girded with truth, and we always don God's righteousness as a breastplate. Our feet are fitted with the preparation of the gospel, and we carry the shield of faith. On our heads, we are protected by the helmet of salvation, and we never cease praying. We are the warriors of the Kingdom of God, and all of heaven is supporting us as we continue to stand.

Chapter 8

Our Miracle Working God!

We have explored various circumstances where the Holy Angels of God, or the Heavenly Host, have manifested to assist us human beings.

In the story of Jacob, we marvel at the extraordinary intervention provided by the angelic hosts. Three angels appeared as five hundred men at four different intervals, terrifying Esau and changing his intentions to kill his brother. Instead, he greeted him in peace.

Consider this: If three angels could appear as 2,000 men, all equipped for battle, then when we say there are more with us than with them, it's mind-boggling. If three angels had the ability to appear as 2,000 men, what else could they disguise themselves as?

When we hear stories of the Six-Day War in Israel, we learn that two Israeli tanks resembled hundreds of tanks from the enemy's perspective. Do you think they might have had some angelic assistance?

Jacob found himself in a life-and-death struggle. Yet, he was confident that God was calling him to return home. He knew God had plans for him, promising to make him into a great nation. So, despite the dangers of the night, the clarity of God's promises was a beacon of hope that shone brightly. He is a great example for us as we hold on to the promises of God.

> *...The effectual fervent prayers of a righteous man availeth much.*
> *James 5:16*

When you fight for your family, your health, or whatever the need may be, God sends angelic help to support you in your struggles. How many times are angels assisting us or protecting us without our knowledge? We see the outcome but may never know the details of how it unfolds.

I once had a similar experience. A miracle happened with the angels, yet I still struggle to comprehend how it all unfolded. What I know is the utterly unexplainable result. Allow me to share the details with.

In 1993, on a cold winter evening, I was driving with two of my children along a dark, narrow, two-lane country road. I was oblivious to the black ice hidden beneath my car, mistakenly believing it was just rain. I was completely unaware of the sudden drop in temperature outside. As I approached a curve on a hill, I gently tapped my brakes. That was when it became clear that I was driving on ice.

A tractor-trailer approached from the opposite direction. Suddenly, my car was completely out of control, sliding sideways on the ice and heading straight into the path of the oncoming semi. I found myself staring face-to-face with the other driver. Everything felt like it was happening in slow motion. My first thought was, "I'm going to heaven!" I could see the impact coming, and there wasn't anything I could do about it. At that moment, I yelled, "Jesus! Jesus! Jesus!"

Then, something completely inexplicable and beyond human understanding happened. After the loud, jarring initial impact of the two vehicles crashing into each other, my car somehow bounced off the front of the truck and slid down the entire length of its trailer. I will never know how my car went from being in front of the truck to being alongside the trailer. The fact that the trailer didn't sway back and forth, zigzagging on the road, killing me, was an absolute miracle. How in the world did that happen?

The front tire on the driver's side of my car was gone. The metal frame of the car was digging into the pavement below. The impact destroyed the front of my vehicle up to where I was sitting. Really? The front end of the car was wrecked, but I was not injured. All the glass in the driver's side window was shattered and embedded in my scalp, yet it never broke the skin.

After sliding alongside the trailer, my car was still on the road and out of my control. It had no steering capability, yet it veered to the right, crashing into a dirt embankment. It finally slid to a stop. God knew I feared hitting something or someone else if the car continued sliding uncontrollably. When my car finally came to an abrupt halt, I was still calling out the name of Jesus repeatedly. My son tapped me on the shoulder and said, "Mom, Mom, you can stop calling for Jesus; we've stopped, and we're all ok!"

Since the driver's side of the car was crushed, the children and I managed to climb out of the wreckage on the passenger side. Miraculously, none of us were hurt! Since we were not injured, my next instinct was to assist the truck driver. The pavement was so slick that I couldn't even stand. We had to move to a grassy area to reach the spot where the truck had stopped.

The kids and I trudged through the icy grass to get to the trucker, who was surrounded by people who had stopped. I'm sure there was plenty of debris on the road. He was in shock. I explained that I was a nurse and asked him if he was injured. He told me, "I'm okay, but I'm sure I killed the other driver." I responded, "No! That was me!" He couldn't comprehend. He asked me to explain and to repeat myself several times. He was utterly amazed to find that I was not dead!

How could that possibly happen? None of it made sense. It defied our understanding of the natural world. I should have died in that accident. Why didn't I?

The impact broke the front axle of the semi, making it undriveable. So, the trucker's company sent a van to pick us both up and drive us back to the nearest town. None of us even thought of going to the hospital. On the way back, the truck driver was able to share what he had just experienced.

He said that his trailer was loaded to the max with steel. He continued, "I kept hearing a voice say, 'Don't break, you'll decapitate her! Don't break! Don't break!" He said, "I heard it over and over and over again."

Angels were in his truck, instructing him on how to navigate this emergency. Where else could those voices have come from? Angels must be why the impact didn't go any further into the car. How did the demolition stop precisely where I was sitting? Angels were there to save us all! How did my car veer off into the dirt embankment without any steering capability? All of it was supernatural! You must admit, not many people can say they've had a head-on collision with a semi and walked away unharmed.

The angels were already there. I didn't need to call and wait for them to arrive from heaven. They were already in my car with me and in the truck with the other driver. How many times have we experienced an unexplainable outcome in our lives? Is it due to the angels? We don't know. We're just like Jacob—he didn't know either.

I am convinced that when I cried out to the Lord, the angels intervened to prevent the trailer from jackknifing and possibly decapitating me. What was the enemy's intention for me at that moment? Since he is the one who comes to kill, steal, and destroy, did the enemy have a different outcome in mind for me?

One more thing to consider: my children and I were listening to worship music right before this accident. Were we already participating in a form of spiritual warfare? Worship acts as a powerful tool in our spiritual battles. It's part of submitting to God, which causes the devil to flee.

Just as the angels showed up for all these Bible characters, they show up for us today.

> *Jesus Christ is [eternally changeless, always] the same yesterday and today and forever. We can trust him to be who he says that he is, and to do what he says he will do. Heb. 13:8 Amp.*

Secret: Worship is a form of warfare!

God's army is available to us just as it was to Jacob, Daniel, Hannah, and Elisha. If three angels can appear as two thousand men, and two tanks can look like hundreds or even thousands to our enemies, then the same miraculous power is accessible to us. Knowing that we have an angelic force behind us is crucial for navigating the maze of the end times.

Each of the characters we have encountered so far drew angelic assistance through their words/prayers. Daniel reviewed Jeremiah's scroll and recognized that the Babylonian captivity was coming to an end. Deeply devoted to God, he fasted and prayed. Gabriel brought him an answer only after Michael fought in heaven, emphasizing the necessity for powerful angels to fight for us. There's undoubtedly more happening around us than meets the eye!

Like Daniel, sometimes answers to our prayers are delayed. God is always teaching us patience. I know He's doing that for me.

In chapter three, angelic warfare aided Hannah as she called on the Lord of Hosts, the Captain of the Angel Armies. Afflicted by an adversary, God sent His host to assist her in response to her prayers. Similarly, Sarah conceived only after a visit from the angels.

We need to remember that when the heavens and the earth were created, God was here on this planet with His divine counsel. We'll learn more about that in later chapters. They are His unseen family and are fellow servants with you and me. We support one another. They are God's children, just as we are God's children.

When Elisha was surrounded by the enemy, the angelic forces were already present to assist him and Israel in their battles. We observed similar armies here on our land; they are already present. We learned that angels have the ability to blind the enemy and to hide us in plain sight!

Hopefully, these stories have caused your expectations to grow. When we understand that our spiritual family members are always there to support us, our faith will begin to speak, "Father, I need help; I need some assistance. I am in a situation that I can't handle, I surrender to your plan."

Just as the Syrian army was blinded, there are similar happenings reported in enemy prison camps. The prisoners were stripped naked and forbidden to take anything into the prison camp, but one woman refused to let go of her Bible. She simply wrapped it in her arms and held it close to her chest. She managed to get through the line while all the soldiers watched, and no one noticed or tried to stop her. It's amazing how God provided for her to take the Word of God with her into her captivity.

In Psalms 35, David asked God to deal with those who plotted his hurt. There are people who will devise your harm or scheme against you. They may devise ways to harm you in the future. David knew to call on God. Because of Jesus, we have even greater access to Him today to ask for Him to confound and shame those who seek after our souls, to turn them back and confuse them.

You have Christ within you! So when the enemy attacks you, they are attacking the God of Heaven. You are His child, and He takes it personally when the enemy comes against you.

> *Let them be as chaff before the wind: and let the angel of the LORD chase them. Let their way be dark and slippery: and let the angel of the LORD persecute them. Ps. 35:5-6*

David asked the angels to persecute the enemy. Now, let's see how that same principle demonstrated itself for Israel under King Hezekiah. We'll begin to unfold this story in 2 Kings 19. You'll also find his story in Isaiah 37.

> *When the king heard them say concerning Tirhakah king of Ethiopia, "Behold, he has come out to make war against you," he sent messengers again to Hezekiah, saying, "Say this to Hezekiah*

> *king of Judah, 'Do not let your God on whom you rely deceive you by saying, "Jerusalem shall not be handed over to the king of Assyria." Listen, you have heard what the Assyrian kings have done to all the lands, destroying them completely. So, will you be spared? 2 Kings. 19:9-11 Amp.*

Assyria had been threatening war with Israel for some time. Now, they have sent a letter to state their intentions. This letter is a direct challenge to the God of Israel. It is from a prideful king who believes he is superior to every nation and every god. The difference is that the God of Israel is alive!

> *Did the gods of the nations whom my forefathers destroyed rescue them--Gozan and Haran [of Mesopotamia] and Rezeph and the people of Eden who were in Telassar? Where is the king of Hamath, the king of Arpad [of northern Syria], the king of the city of Sepharvaim, and of Hena and Ivvah?'" 2 Ki 10 12-13 Amp.*

These are threats from the enemy. They come in the form of words! Words instill fear! Hezekiah laid out the threat before God, engaging in spiritual warfare. He knew he could not fight and win in the natural, so he battled in a way his enemy could not comprehend. He placed his trust in the God of Israel. The enemy doesn't understand this kind of warfare. Hezekiah put his trust in Yahweh.

> *In God have I put my trust and confident reliance; I will not be afraid. What can man do to me? Ps.56:11*

The word Fear means frightened, afraid, and dread; it is envisioning the outcome as being terrible. We must keep dreading out of our thoughts.

I love this next part.

> *Hezekiah received the letter from the hand of the messengers and read it. Then he went up to the house (temple) of the LORD and spread it out before the LORD. 2 Ki 19:14*

That's what we need to do. If it takes writing down your fears and laying them before God, then do it. That's why I keep a journal. If someone is speaking negatively about you, or if something terrible is starting to happen, then write it down and lay it out before the Lord.

If you receive a letter from the IRS, lay it before the Lord. If your bank account decreases, lay it before the Lord. If it feels like your life is falling apart, write it down and say, "Here it is Father; please see, hear, and act on my behalf. Send your angels to assist me."

> *Hezekiah prayed (warfare) before the LORD and said, "O LORD, the God of Israel, who is enthroned above the cherubim [of the ark in the temple], You are the God, You alone, of all the kingdoms of the earth. You have made the heavens and the earth. 2 Ki 19:15 Amp.*

He first acknowledges the greatness of his King. He magnifies him, just as we are instructed by Yeshua when he teaches us the "Lord's Prayer." We begin by recognizing who God is and His immense power.

He acknowledges that His God is alive and the only true God. All the other nations that have perished did not have a God like our God.

> *O LORD, bend down Your ear and hear; LORD, open Your eyes and see; hear the [taunting] words of Sennacherib, which he has sent to taunt and defy the living God. 2 Ki 19:16 Amp.*

Remember who else said that? David said it when he faced Goliath. "Who is this uncircumcised Philistine that he should defy the armies of the living God?" Now Hezekiah is saying the same thing. Those words worked for David, and they resonate for Hezekiah, and they will also work for you.

Hezekiah is asking God to take this personally. When we say the battle belongs to the Lord, that's what we mean; let him take it personally on your behalf.

Proclaim, "I am your child; do you see what they are doing?

Secret: The enemy shows no fear in insulting God. Respond as Hezekiah did!

The enemy is insulting and falsely accusing the God of Israel! He is saying our God is like all the other false gods that have no power to save. This enemy does not know who he is dealing with. I dare say that there are many things going on in the earth today, and the powers that be have no idea who they are dealing with. Yahweh is not like the other Gods of the earth.

> *It is true, LORD, that the Assyrian kings have devastated the nations and their lands and have thrown their gods into the fire, for they were not [real] gods but [only] the work of men's hands, wood and stone. So, they [could destroy them and] have destroyed them. Now, O LORD our God, please, save us from his hand so that all the kingdoms of the earth may know [without any doubt] that You alone, O LORD, are God." 2 Ki. 19:17-19 Amp.*

The prophet Isaiah is absent during Hezekiah's prayer, but he is still attuned to God's response to Hezekiah. At times, God may choose to involve another person to convey His answers. When we are overwhelmed by fear or distress, we might struggle to perceive God's guidance independently. Nonetheless, God always listens to us and will offer an answer, regardless of the circumstances.

> *Then Isaiah the son of Amoz sent word to Hezekiah, saying, "Thus says the LORD, the God of Israel: 'I have heard your prayer to Me regarding Sennacherib king of Assyria. This is the word that the LORD has spoken against him: 'The virgin daughter of Zion Has despised you and mocked you; The daughter of Jerusalem Has shaken her head behind you! 'Whom have you taunted and blasphemed? Against whom have you raised your voice, And haughtily lifted up your eyes? Against the Holy One of Israel! 2 Ki 19:20-22*

God is saying, "You haven't just attacked Hezekiah and My people, but you attacked Me personally." What do you suspect He might do?

> *'Through your messengers you have taunted and defied the Lord, And have said [boastfully], "With my many chariots I came up to the heights of the mountains, To the remotest parts of Lebanon; I cut down its tall cedar trees and its choicest cypress trees. I entered its most distant lodging, its densest forest. "I dug wells and drank foreign waters, And with the sole of my feet I dried up All the rivers of [the Lower Nile of] Egypt." 'Have you not heard [asks the God of Israel]? Long ago I did it; From ancient times I planned it. Now I have brought it to pass, That you [king of Assyria] should [be My instrument to] turn fortified cities into ruinous heaps. 2 Ki. 19:23-25 Amp.*

God is telling Sennacherib, "The reason for your success in battle is because of Me." God has used him as a tool of correction.

> *'Therefore their inhabitants were powerless, They were shattered [in spirit] and put to shame; They were like plants of the field, the green herb, As grass on the housetops is scorched before it is grown up. 'But I [the LORD] know your sitting down [O Sennacherib], Your going out, your coming in, And your raging against Me. 'Because of your raging against Me, And because your arrogance and complacency have come up to My ears, I will put My hook in your nose, And My bridle in your lips, And I will turn you back [to Assyria] by the way that you came. 2 Ki. 19:26-28 Amp.*

God is angry for the sake of his people and for the arrogance of Sennacherib. He is saying, "I heard what you said!" The scripture tells us that we will be accountable for every word we have spoken! Sennacherib has raged against the one true and living God!

> *'Then this shall be the sign [of these things] to you [Hezekiah]: this year you will eat what grows of itself, in the second year what springs up voluntarily, and in the third year sow and reap, plant vineyards, and eat their fruit. 2 Ki 19:29*

This threatening letter came in the Shmita year, which takes place every seven years in Israel. Isiah assures Hezekiah that he will be present for the upcoming harvest. During the Shmita year, planting or harvesting is not permitted. The following year, they can consume what grows naturally. After that, they may sow, reap, and plant vineyards. In this, God assures Hezekiah that they will not go into captivity because he will still be here for the next harvest.

> *The survivors who remain of the house of Judah will again take root downward and bear fruit upward. For a remnant will go forth from Jerusalem, and [a band of] survivors from Mount Zion. The zeal of the LORD of hosts shall perform this. 2 Ki 19:3-31 Amp.*

The God of angel armies is about to deploy His forces to win this battle. He will confront the boastful arrogance of the enemies of Judah.

> *'Therefore thus says the LORD concerning the king of Assyria: He will not come to this city [Jerusalem] nor shoot an arrow there; nor will he come before it with a shield nor throw up a siege ramp against it. By the way that he came, by the same way he will return, and he will not come into this city,'" declares the LORD. For **I will protect** this city to save it, for My own sake and for My servant David's sake.'" Then it came to pass that night, that the **angel** of the LORD went forth and struck down 185,000 [men] in the camp of the Assyrians; when the survivors got up early in the morning, behold, all [185,000] of them were dead. 2 Ki 19:32-35 Amp.*

Hallelujah! Judah didn't have to lift a finger. We see repeatedly in the scriptures that God says He will go with us or that He will go before us in battle. At times, Israel still had to fight, but not this time. The battle truly was the Lord's! One angel was sent out to destroy 185,000 men. Who is this angel? He is called "The Angel of the Lord!' Is this Messiah Himself?

It only took one angel to eliminate 185,000 soldiers! No wonder Elisha said there are more with us than with them! How can we possibly believe we are alone or outnumbered in our battles?

> *So Sennacherib king of Assyria left and returned home, and lived at Nineveh. 2 Ki 19:36*

Then this is what happened to him:

> *It came about as he was worshiping in the house of Nisroch his god, that his sons Adrammelech and Sharezer killed him with a sword; and they escaped to the land of Ararat. And Esarhaddon his son became king in his place. 2 Ki 19:37*

Wow! There are consequences for our actions, just as we've seen in all our previous studies. In response to the passionate and fervent prayer of a righteous man, the angels acted. This theme appears throughout the scriptures. We often fail to understand the strength and power of our God, who He is, and that He will stop at nothing to rescue His beloved.

So how many angels does it take to kill 185,000 warriors? Maybe 5? 10? Maybe one!

Consider this: when the tribes of Israel escaped from Egypt during the Exodus, they marched in regiments according to their tribes, each carrying a banner. When God called them forth, He referred to them as His Army. The children of God were an army then and we are an army now!

> *And it came to pass the selfsame day, that the LORD did bring the children of Israel out of the land of Egypt by their armies. Ex. 12:51*

God saw them as an army, prepared for war and ready to fight. We are also expected to be ready for battles every day. Matthew expresses it this way:

> *And from the days of John the Baptist until now the kingdom of heaven suffereth violence, and the violent take it by force. Matt. 11:12*

Secret: The violent take it by force!

We shouldn't be on the defensive all the time, constantly trying to defend ourselves. Instead, we should be ready to reclaim what the devil has stolen from the Kingdom of God.

> *He that committeth sin is of the devil; for the devil sinneth from the beginning. For this purpose the Son of God was manifested, that he might destroy the works of the devil. 1 Jn 3:8*

Yeshua came to destroy the works of the devil. He now lives in you. His commission within you is the same as His. It is to destroy the works of the devil. We are living in incredible corruption right now. Satan is manifesting his agenda openly and in your face. We may feel like Lot whose soul was vexed daily by living in such filth.

> *And delivered just Lot, vexed with the filthy conversation of the wicked: (For that righteous man dwelling among them, in seeing and hearing, **vexed** his righteous soul from day to day with their unlawful deeds;) The Lord knoweth how to deliver the godly out of temptations, and to reserve the unjust unto the day of judgment to be punished: 2 Pe 2:7-9*

Secret: If you participate in the things of this world, it will vex your soul!

I had to rebuke the spirit of despair after watching a short video clip from the Grammy Awards. It hurt my soul for my King. You and I are very different. We are set apart as the Bride of Christ. We must guard our eyes and ears to navigate the days of Sodom and Gomorrah in which we are living.

Hezekiah was one of the few Godly Kings of Israel. He knew how to take his fears to the only one who could rescue him and his land from the enemy.

> *The Lord is on my side; I will not fear: what can man do unto me?*
> *Ps. 118:6*

We will need to remember this in the coming days. The angels respond to our words. Instead of speaking his fears, Hezekiah took the threatening letter of the enemy directly to God and laid it out before Him. The angels are waiting to act for you as well.

Chapter 9

A Redeemer in Israel!

I mentioned that I have a habit of asking many questions. So here are a few more: Do we understand that we are the Bride of Christ? Do we truly grasp what that means? If so, what is necessary to prepare ourselves? Why is it important for us to recognize that we have the army of God supporting us in these last days?

We are living in very dark times. The battle lines have been drawn. Every day, people choose which side to support. Just look at the recent Grammy presentation, and you'll see clear signs of those who openly proclaim to be followers of God's archenemy, Satan.

I have heard the objection that seeking out angels is dangerous. This is a complete misconception. We are not trying to connect with an angel; if that becomes your goal, your focus is incorrect. Our relationship is with Yeshua/Jesus. Angels are readily available to those of us who are heirs of salvation, and this is part of our inheritance. It saddens me to think that a believer would be afraid of our fellow servants in the kingdom of God, the Heavenly Host.

Satan has a counterfeit for everything—even angels. Your duty is to abide under the shadow of the Almighty, to know His voice, and to sense His direction. We must remain in the Word of God; when we do that, we will not ever be deceived by an "angel of light."

We must test every spirit, which includes what we see and hear with our spiritual eyes and ears. Many of us have developed our senses to distinguish good from evil. Over the decades, we have spent time in the presence of God. This process does not happen overnight; it requires diligence and commitment.

Secret: Soaking in the presence of God sharpens your spiritual senses.

In the scriptures, we see many men who fall or faint in the presence of an angelic being, and rightly so. They are powerful and glorious. However, most of us don't have the same level of calling on our lives as John the Revelator, Isaiah, or Ezekiel. Their heavenly encounters were so profound that their physical bodies could not withstand the presence of these angelic beings.

There are various kinds of angels that manifest in different forms. The significance of their mission or the message they convey seems to affect the power they exude.

From a personal standpoint, I have had only two encounters where I couldn't move or look up due to the presence of the Glory of the Master. However, there have been many instances where I was granted the privilege of catching a glimpse into the other side. Those experiences were incredibly tender, merciful, and kind. I never want to take these moments for granted, and I am eternally grateful for them. I don't believe there's anything unusual about my walk with Yeshua/Jesus. To me, this is the normal Christian life. As the Bride of the Messiah, we should seek His presence daily. The supernatural is simply a part of belonging to His Heavenly Kingdom.

Secret: Being a Christian is supernatural! Do you realize that?

I must trust God just as you do, to test every spirit and discern what is of God and what is not. I don't think it's necessary for us to walk around in fear of being deceived if we are immersing ourselves in the Word regularly, which is Yeshua himself. Greater is He who is in you than he who is in the world. Sometimes, we forget who is living inside us.

I want to remind you that God has both a seen family and an unseen family, and we were created to work together. Don't deny them access out of fear. They are present whether you see them or not. They are working among you and for you.

The world is full of demonic influences. They are no longer hiding; they're right in your face. Just watch the evening news broadcast on TV and try to endure the commercials. Much of our entertainment industry has openly pledged their loyalty to Satan. They show no shame and are leading many naive, unwarned people to hell with them. That is what Satan does; he deceives and leads astray, especially the unbelievers.

It's concerning that Christians often participate in activities that don't align with the Kingdom of God and their professed identity. They assure themselves that it's harmless simply because it's legal or widespread in our culture. Here in America, we've embraced the concept of grace so deeply that many believe that just recognizing God and His existence is enough for eternal life. That is not scriptural!

That is not enough! Even Satan himself believes and trembles. However, much of mankind is not that smart. They don't even tremble over the power and awe of God! They are ignorant of the righteousness of a Holy God and what's required to be part of the remnant.

> *You believe that there is one God. You do well. Even the demons believe—and tremble! Jms. 2:19*

The part of humanity that is not trembling doesn't realize that this is a "Holy God." To worship a Holy God and be part of His eternal Kingdom requires being a set-apart people. It requires that you become holy as He is holy.

Secret: Understanding the Holiness of God will cause you to tremble.

> *....Be ye holy; for I am holy. 1 Peter 1:16*

But ye are a chosen generation, a royal priesthood, an holy nation, a peculiar people; that ye should shew forth the praises of him who hath called you out of darkness into his marvellous light; 1 Pe 2:9

God would not tell us to be holy if it were not achievable. Each day, I notice the path to eternity becoming increasingly narrow. In larger families, there is often just one individual completely devoted to God. The Elect and the remnant are being sealed for God's everlasting kingdom. The divide between good and evil is widening, and we may soon face isolation within our families or social circles because of our beliefs.

Secret: At times, being separated from family or social circles can be a blessing.

Recently, while praying for my daughter, I asked God for a protective shield to surround her. Suddenly, I heard a loud clanging noise. I exclaimed, "Whoa! What was that?" Before an answer could come, I saw a massive, armored circular wall being put in place. It completely surrounded her on every side and appeared impenetrable! This happened so quickly that I nearly missed it. I have come to lovingly call this a "flash vision." I realized that as soon as I prayed, God answered and even allowed me to witness in the spirit the protective shield being put in place.

This is part of exercising our senses. This is happening to all of God's children, but not everyone has learned to listen yet. Trust that things are occurring for you in God's Kingdom, even if you don't hear or see anything. Everything He does is for your good.

The path to destruction has grown quite wide, yet the path to the kingdom has become even more narrow. I saw this in a vision. It was clear that very few people were on this narrow road, leaving great spaces between them. They weren't walking together anymore. Many were walking alone and feeling isolated. Many people have already fallen off the narrow road because they have become enamored with the world. In my youth, this path seemed crowded to me, with many people walking side by side and holding hands, but that's no longer the case.

> *"Enter through the narrow gate. For wide is the gate and broad and easy to travel is the path that leads the way to destruction and eternal loss, and there are many who enter through it. But small is the gate and narrow and **difficult to travel** is the path that leads the way to [everlasting] life, and there are few who find it. Matt. 7:13-14 Amp.*

The notion that we should strive to live a holy life because Yeshua is holy is not a widely accepted viewpoint, even within Christian circles. However, there is a remnant, and there is The Elect! They will be holy just as He is holy. He is preparing a bride without spot or blemish.

We must make decisions based on following our King and not being coerced or persuaded by others to waver. It's time now to get your feet planted firmly in the presence of the King, bowing to no one else.

It's important to remember that you are not alone. Experiencing supernatural encounters shouldn't be unusual for God's people; they should occur in a normal Christian life. We are meant to perceive things spiritually; it's normal to experience the presence of angels. We are all of one family. We humans are created in the image of God himself. We are His image bearers in this life. He intended for us to **rule** and **take dominion** in this realm. He established this in Eden, and it is His intention for us to return to that position of authority. We begin in a garden, and we will finish in a garden.

The enemy has tried to convince us that he is the one in control and that we are powerless. However, we are not powerless! We are dressed and equipped for war. Not only do we walk in a powerful anointing from on high, but we've also been given assistance from the invisible world. We are not alone.

You and I are a sacred space. For those of us who have studied the Tabernacle in the wilderness or the Temple, we understand the immense holiness associated with it. We recognize that the utensils are holy, the incense is holy, the ground is holy, and the furniture is holy. It served as the dwelling place of God on earth. There is a deep sense of reverence to it all.

The same sacredness once attributed to the Temple on earth is now attributed to you. We have become sacred space! We are the dwelling place for the Most High God. He lives in us. You have become the Ark of the New Covenant! Our lives must begin to reflect the holiness of the One within.

> *What? know ye not that your body is the temple of the Holy Ghost which is in you, which ye have of God, and ye are not your own? 1 Cor. 6:19*

There is a separation, a setting apart that is happening. We can no longer be part of what the world has to offer. The days of fence-sitting are over. We're either for Him or against Him.

> *And Elijah came unto all the people, and said, How long halt ye between two opinions? if the Lord be God, follow him: but if Baal, then follow him. And the people answered him not a word. 1 Kings 18:21*

We must decide. This is where we are. It's showdown time. It's time to get aggressive for the Kingdom and be jealous for God and His Kingdom. We are not alone; we have backup. God has two families, seen and unseen, and we are created to work together to bring about the Kingdom of God here on earth. Remember that the angels danced for joy at the creation of mankind. They love us!

When we look to the end of the age, we see humans in glorified bodies functioning alongside our angelic, divinely created family in unity for God's kingdom. They accompany us, protect us, and assist us in warfare.

This whole life is warfare! Every word we speak is either for or against the outcome of the Kingdom of God!

The completion of our salvation occurs when we exchange these earthly bodies for the glorified bodies that God always intended us to have. We were not created to undertake this life journey alone; we have been given assistance from the supernatural realm.

We are approaching an end. Those of us who are overcomers who have served the Lord with gladness will live eternally in glorified bodies. These people are set apart and marked for God; we will serve the Lord with gladness and share the responsibility with His angelic family.

> *But [we are different, because] our citizenship is in heaven. And from there we eagerly await [the coming of] the Savior, the Lord Jesus Christ; who, by exerting that power which enables Him even to subject everything to Himself, will [not only] transform [but completely refashion] our earthly bodies so that they will be like His glorious resurrected body. Php.3:20-21*

He will refashion our bodies to be like His.

> *And we all, with unveiled face, continually seeing as in a mirror the glory of the Lord, are progressively being transformed into His image from [one degree of] glory to [even more] glory, which comes from the Lord, [who is] the Spirit. 2 Co 3:18*

We are supernatural beings. We currently inhabit earthly bodies, but that is not our ultimate destiny. This life is not our true home. Every day, we are being transformed with each victory we experience, becoming more like Him, moving from one degree of glory to the next.

Secret: You don't realize you are being transformed daily for good or for evil. Embrace that!

The entire Bible essentially chronicles the ongoing conflict between Yahweh and the earthly gods, along with the struggle of Yahweh's followers-Abraham's seed—against nations ruled by these other deities. The objective is to restore the original design of Eden. What was lost in the fall will be redeemed. Until He comes, we occupy and stand. We do that by warfare. Often, we find ourselves engaged in warfare without even realizing it.

Warfare comes in many forms. Your words are constant elements of this warfare, no matter what you say. When you are born again and publicly declare your faith, you have proclaimed your allegiance to Jesus for eternity. Unfortunately, many people do not realize that they were inducted into an army at the moment of conversion. They were unaware that there would be a battle. This is our fault; we didn't train them, and we didn't teach them.

Here are ways we entered into warfare without realizing it:

Secret: Sometimes, we enter into spiritual warfare without realizing it.

Baptism is Warfare:

Your baptism is warfare. You go under the water, leaving behind the world controlled by the enemy. You enter a new kingdom reality. Then you are raised to a new life, surrendering to the King and to his victory in the earthly realm at all costs. We are joining the battle with Him by our side until His Kingdom comes on earth as it is in heaven. You have pledged your allegiance to the King, Yeshua, through this baptism. You are equipped and weaponized for war.

Communion is Warfare:

Communion (The Lord's Supper) is another form of warfare. Every time you partake of the Lord's body, you recommit to Him and to fight for Him in this life. It's like a renewal of vows each time you partake. Being intentional when you take communion will boost your confidence in warfare. It serves as an outward sealing of what you know He has accomplished for you through His death and resurrection.

Once more, you have embraced the blood and integrated it into your life. Each time you partake of His body and blood, you make a public declaration. This act serves as a symbol; you are expressing your dedication to Him, your purpose for living, and your commitment to the fight.

Worship is Warfare:

Worship is warfare. The enemy despises the glorification of Yeshua and is angered by reminders of what the blood has purchased for us.

> *Submit yourselves, therefore, to God. Resist the devil, and he will flee from you. Jms. 4:7*

Worship is the greatest submission one can offer to God. It repulses the devil! There are many more weapons in our warfare arsenal. However, these are foundational ones that every Christian engages in without realizing these activities are acts of war in the eyes of the enemy.

Angels often appear in the Bible in response to prayer and in praise. However, it suggests that we may entertain angels without even realizing it. Therefore, it's possible for angelic beings to take on human form, and we might not recognize them. We see this happening in scripture.

> *Do not neglect to extend hospitality to strangers [especially among the family of believers--being friendly, cordial, and gracious, sharing the comforts of your home and doing your part generously], for by this some have entertained angels without knowing it. Heb. 13:2*

A perfect example of this can be found in the Book of Judges. In this story, Israel faced tremendous oppression from the Philistines and prayed continuously for a redeemer. God begins to answer their plea by sending an angel who appears as a man.

> *Now Israel again did what was evil in the sight of the LORD, and the LORD gave them into the hands of the Philistines for forty*

> *years. And there was a certain man of Zorah, of the family of the Danites, whose name was Manoah; and his wife was infertile and had no children. And the Angel of the LORD appeared to the woman and said to her, "Behold, you are infertile and have no children, but you shall conceive and give birth to a son. Jdg 13:1-3*

An angel appears! Once again, this is the Angel of the Lord! Do you think this woman has been in constant prayer about her barrenness? We know that Israel is crying out for a redeemer, and now, here comes an angel to bring hope. There are similarities in this story to Hannah's ordeal. Once more, we are looking at the salvation of God's people who have strayed and are experiencing oppression from the enemy.

> *Therefore, be careful not to drink wine or [any other] intoxicating drink, and do not eat anything [ceremonially] unclean. For behold, you shall conceive and give birth to a son. No razor shall come upon his head, for the boy shall be a Nazirite [dedicated] to God from birth; and he shall begin to rescue Israel from the hands of the Philistines." Jdg. 13:4-5*

This child is to be dedicated to God from birth. However, Israel has already faced persecution from the Philistines for forty years. This means there are still many more years of hardship to endure before the child matures. Just like Hannah, this woman is not informed that her son will be a redeemer.

Israel will have to wait until he reaches his teenage years to witness the incredible strength that God has bestowed upon this child. He can confront many of the Philistines all on his own. God is sending a redeemer. The angel has arrived in response to the prayers of a nation and a woman in distress. Angels come because of our words!

> *Then the woman went and told her husband, saying, "A Man of God came to me and his appearance was like the appearance of*

> *the Angel of God, very awesome. I did not ask Him where he came from, and he did not tell me his name. Jdg. 13:6*

She calls him a man. She thinks he looks like an angel, but she's not certain, so she refers to him as a man. He seems awesome. She didn't ask him where he came from. Usually, when you see an angel, you don't think about what questions you need to ask. She doesn't know for sure if he's from God, but there's something truly remarkable about him and what he's saying.

> *But He said to me, 'Behold, you shall conceive and give birth to a son, and now you shall not drink wine or [any other] intoxicating drink, nor eat anything [ceremonially] unclean, for the boy shall be a Nazirite to God from birth to the day of his death.'" Jdg. 13:7*

She chooses to believe this "man," who says that she is going to have a son and that he will be set apart to God from his birth. This angel simply appears. That is how it works. They are already present, and at some point, they reveal themselves to us. Remember, just because you don't see them doesn't mean they aren't there. They are always present!

> *Then Manoah pleaded with the LORD and said, "O Lord, please let the Man of God whom You sent come again to us and teach us what we are to do for the boy who is to be born." Jdg. 13:8*

Since Manoah doesn't realize that this is an angel, he refers to him as a man of God. However, they are confident that this man is sent from God.

The word "plead" is to Intreat the Lord: It means to worship, that is to intercede and to reciprocate by listening.

Prayer encompasses both listening and speaking. He is asking God for the angel, who he thinks is a man, to return. It is not wrong to request clarity from God, who can provide it in any way He chooses. This reflects Manoah's sincere desire to comprehend what God has promised and what actions they need to take to remain obedient. This is their heartfelt intention. The couple genuinely wants to stay obedient.

> *And God listened to the voice of Manoah; and the Angel of God came again to the woman as she sat in the field, but Manoah her husband was not with her. So the woman ran quickly and told her husband, "Behold, the Man who came to me the other day has appeared to me." Then Manoah got up and followed his wife, and came to the Man and said to him, "Are you the Man who spoke to this woman?" He said, "I am." Jdg. 13:9-11*

Secret: Angels are patient. They will wait for you.

The angel waited for Manoah to come. We often see the patience of our fellow servants (angels) throughout the scripture. They will wait. They stay till a meal is made or an offering is presented. They are not in a hurry. They are here on assignment for you.

> *And Manoah said, "Now when your words come true, what shall be the boy's manner of life, and his vocation?" The Angel of the LORD said to Manoah, "The woman must pay attention to everything that I said to her. She may not eat anything that comes from the vine nor drink wine or [any other] intoxicating drink, nor eat anything [ceremonially] unclean. She shall observe everything that I commanded her." Then Manoah said to the Angel of the LORD, "Please let us detain you and let us prepare a young goat for you [to eat]." The Angel of the LORD said to Manoah, "Though you detain me, I will not eat your food, but if you prepare a burnt offering, offer it to the LORD." For Manoah did not know that he was the Angel of the LORD. Jdg. 13:12-16*

Manoah still doesn't realize that this is an angel. Think about this: you may have already entertained an angel unaware.

> *Manoah said to the Angel of the LORD, "What is your name, so that when your words come true, we may honor you?" Jdg. 13:17*

This angel seeks no honor. He desires no recognition. There are only a few instances in scripture where we are given the name of an angel.

> *But the Angel of the LORD said to him, "Why do you ask my name, seeing it is wonderful (miraculous)?" Jdg. 13:18*

The Angel's name is Wonderful! Who else is called Wonderful?

> *For to us a Child shall be born, to us a Son shall be given; And the government shall be upon His shoulder, And His name shall be called Wonderful Counselor, Mighty God, Everlasting Father, Prince of Peace. Is. 9:6*

This just makes me go WOW! Think about that! Who might this angel be?

> *So Manoah took the young goat with the grain offering and offered it on the rock to the LORD, and He performed miracles while Manoah and his wife looked on. Jdg. 13:19*

We aren't told what miracle this angel performs only that he is able to do miraculous things.

> *For when the flame went up toward heaven from the altar, the Angel of the LORD ascended in the altar flame. When Manoah and his wife saw this they fell on their faces to the ground. Jdg. 13:20*

There's no doubt they have entertained an angel unawares. This brings me to tears. Can you even imagine the glory, the holiness of this moment? The angel of the Lord is the pre-incarnate Jesus. So many times, in the scriptures, He has lowered Himself to reveal Himself to mankind and to rescue us from the jaws of the enemy. His love for us is beyond human comprehension.

> *The Angel of the LORD did not appear again to Manoah or his wife. Then Manoah knew that he was the Angel of the LORD. So*

> *Manoah said to his wife, "We will certainly die, because we have seen **God**." Jdg. 13:21-22*

They realized that this was a supernatural, divine encounter and that it might even be Yahweh himself. I shared this earlier, but we need to be reminded again here. We learned in studies of the Near East that the Hebrews understood that there were two Yahweh. There was one that you did not see and one that you did. He would appear in the flesh like he did with Abraham before the destruction of Sodom and Gomorrah. He met Abraham and even sat down to share a meal. At times, He took on a human appearance, so they understood that He could assume more than one form.

They believe this is Yahweh Himself. Manoah says, "We're going to die because we saw God." Then his wife responds:

> *But his [sensible] wife said to him, "If the LORD had desired to kill us, He would not have received a burnt offering and a grain offering from our hands, nor would He have shown us all these things, nor would He have announced such things as these at this time." So the woman [in due time] gave birth to a son and named him Samson; and the boy grew and the LORD blessed him. Jdg. 13:23-24*

Samson becomes the deliverer against the Philistines. If you're unfamiliar with the rest of the story, take time to read Judges 14-16. Samson was one of the strongest men to have ever lived.

Secret: You might not recognize that you have been visited by an angel. Ponder that!

We may not always recognize when we encounter a divine being. However, we can be assured that whenever we engage in warfare or intense prayer of any kind, our unseen family is working alongside us to fulfill our Father's will.

Let me share a personal modern-day encounter that I know about. My daughter, Rachel, passed away in 2015. We never found out why. She was just 38 years old when she left us.

When she was in her early twenties, Rachel was on a mission trip with YWAM in Mexico when she lost her wallet and passport. She and her team began to intercede for the wallet to be found. She needed her passport and ID to be able to re-enter the United States.

Secret: Angels help you find things.

Rachel began to retrace her steps through the city where the group had spent the day. She was searching all over the streets when a gentleman spoke to her, asking, "Are you looking for something?" She replied, "Yes, I lost my wallet." He pointed up the street toward a restaurant where Rachel and the team had eaten lunch. He then told her, "It's on the windowsill next to where you were sitting at the restaurant. Everything is still in it." Rachel turned her head to follow the direction in which the man pointed. When she turned back to look at him, he had completely vanished. There was no way this "man" could have disappeared from her sight in seconds. He was an angel!

Rachel ran to the restaurant and there on the windowsill was her wallet and her passport. Nothing was missing. She had just entertained an angel, unaware. They are still here for us. They continue to enjoy assisting you.

The team had done warfare and prayer on Rachel's behalf, and our loving Father chose to send her assistance in the form of an angel. Our God is an awesome God!

Chapter 10

The Breakout Angel!

The disciples of Jesus were well-acquainted with the presence of angels. Just think back to the angels at the tomb during the resurrection! Their ministry didn't end there; they continued to make appearances throughout the New Testament, and the Book of Revelation is brimming with them.

What are your thoughts on how these angels supported believers in spiritual warfare after Jesus's ascension? So, let's take a look. In the Book of Acts, we encounter King Herod, who seeks to gain favor with the Jews. This appears to be yet another political maneuver. He believes the most effective way to achieve this is by targeting the disciple Peter, so he arrests and imprisons him.

> *When he had seized Peter, he put him in prison, turning him over to four squads of soldiers of four each to guard him [in rotation throughout the night], planning after the Passover to bring him out before the people [for execution]. Acts. 12:4*

They planned to kill Peter after Passover. We often see politics play out this way even today in our own country. People are betrayed and sacrificed for others' political gain.

> *So Peter was kept in prison, but fervent and persistent prayer for him was being made to God by the church. Acts. 12:5*

Intercession and warfare represented a continuous, unceasing prayer. Peter was a prominent brother among the believers. He was greatly beloved, and the saints feared for his life.

> *The very night before Herod was to bring him forward, Peter was sleeping between two soldiers, bound with two chains, and sentries were in front of the door guarding the prison. Acts.12:6*

I find it interesting that Peter is sleeping. He isn't awake, tossing and turning. He isn't crying. He's sleeping, but the church is praying.

> *Suddenly, an angel of the Lord appeared [beside him] and a light shone in the cell. The angel struck Peter's side and awakened him, saying, "Get up quickly!" And the chains fell off his hands. Acts. 12:7*

This reminds me of the song we sing about Jesus being a chain-breaking Savior!

> *The angel said to him, "Prepare yourself and strap on your sandals [to get ready for whatever may happen]." And he did so. Then the angel told him, "Put on your robe and follow me." And Peter went out following the angel. He did not realize that what was being done by the angel was real, but thought he was seeing a vision. When they had passed the first guard and the second, they came to the iron gate that leads into the city. Of its own accord it swung open for them; and they went out and went along one street, and at once the angel left him. Acts. 12:8-10*

Secret: Angels give us ways to escape!

The angel has accomplished his goal. He freed Peter and got him out of prison. This angel guided him. Just like in physical battles, the angels go before us. The church was in a spiritual battle praying for Peter, and an angel came to guide Peter out of the prison and out of the city. What happened in Sodom and Gomorrah? The angels actually took Lot by the hand and led him out of the city.

The Angel only went as far as necessary with Peter to grant him his freedom. The door swung open on its own. I can't even imagine how heavy that massive city gate must have been, yet it opened by itself. It reminds me of the huge temple doors that would never stay closed but opened every night after the resurrection of Jesus.

If you remember, the temple doors would not stay closed at night after the resurrection. So amazing! The Priest closed them every night, yet each morning, they would find them open again. Do you think maybe there was an angel involved in that?

> *When Peter came to his senses, he said, "Now I know for certain that the Lord has **sent His angel** and has rescued me from the hand of Herod and from all that the Jewish people were expecting [to do to me]." Acts. 12;11 Amp.*

The Jews plotted to kill Peter, but God had a different plan. Hallelujah. He is a deliverer. The angel was sent in response to the church's prayers and intercession for Peter. The plans of the enemy had no power over him.

> *Behold, I give unto you power to tread on serpents and scorpions, and over all the power of the enemy: and nothing shall by any means hurt you. Luke 10:19*

The serpents and scorpions represent Satan and his demons.

Secret: As a believer in Jesus, you have power over ALL the power of the enemy!

I can relate to this story because I also had an angel come to my rescue. This one stands out in my mind when I think of the Roman soldier. It was the first time I saw an angel in battle attire. I don't believe I've seen one dressed like that since. He was wearing the garb of a Roman soldier.

I was to be a bridesmaid at my best friend's wedding in Tulsa, Oklahoma, in the late '70s. Joe and I were a young married couple with a single income. Attending the wedding was a stretch for us, not only financially. We had four little children at home.

My friend Dianna had booked rooms for us at a local hotel, but we couldn't find it. We had never been in this city before and didn't know our way around. Those were the days before cell phones and GPS. So, Joe and I stopped and rented a room at a nearby motel. We checked in and weren't there long before demonic activity began to manifest in the room.

I guess this was a transit motel that had many hourly guests instead of nightly ones because the things we saw in that room were horrendous. I wanted to leave the motel, but we had already paid for the night. What was I going to tell the clerk? That room is full of demons! Do you think he would have believed me?

I wouldn't have any problem doing that today, but I wasn't as bold as I needed to be in my youth. Remember, Joe and I were in the deliverance ministry. We understood what we were dealing with, but this caught me off guard.

As I looked into the mirror, I could see reflected behind me a horrendous orgy going on. Of course, when I turned around, those images had vanished. I felt I was witnessing a replay of events that had occurred in that room at some earlier time. It took my breath away. I gasped and covered my mouth in horror as I recounted to Joe what I had seen; I had never witnessed anything like this before. We immediately went into battle mode. We prayed in the spirit and commanded the demons to leave. We conducted a spiritual house cleaning in that room, but somehow, I could not unsee what I had experienced. I felt tormented.

What I saw was not only sexual but bizarre, insane, and not conducive to normal human anatomy. I did not think I would be able to fall asleep or stay the night in that room.

Joe held and comforted me as we prayed for the Father to send protection. Just then, it began to rain outside. There was an overhang outside the room where people could walk under it to stay dry. However, no one walked under the overhang in front of our door. Instead, as they approached where we were, they would step back out from under the cover and into the rain until they passed our room. Then they would return, walking under the awning and out of the rain again. It was strange!

Secret: Unbelievers avoid your angels.

Then I saw the reason no one was walking in front of our door. It was because God had summoned an angel. He had placed him outside our door. He was a massive being, dressed in full armor with his weapon drawn. He stood about nine feet tall and was very large in stature. There was only one, but no one dared to approach him. They may not have seen him with their eyes, but they certainly must have sensed his presence. Because they weren't walking anywhere near that door.

I managed to sleep through the night and meet with the wedding party in the morning without being terrified all night long. We had learned early in our walk that we had authority over demons, and the Father had sent us assistance in our warfare. Hallelujah!

We, as God's people, still have a limited understanding of the Unseen realm, but we are learning more each day and expect backup to arrive. We have learned that we are not alone.

David asks YHVH to draw out his spear and to stop those who were persecuting him. That is what that angel did outside my room that night. He drew out his spear.

It states the angel of the Lord encamps round about them that fear him and delivers them.

> *The angel of the LORD encampeth round about them that fear him, and delivereth them. O taste and see that the Lord is good: blessed is the man that trusteth in him Ps. 34:7-8*

The word "encamped" means that the angels pitch a tent; this is their home. They have established a dwelling place, a resting place around **you** because you fear God. They live among us; they are always present. They don't just come and go. They remain with those who revere God. They deliver us, equip us, fight for us, strengthen us, and they are armed.

Many are the afflictions of the righteous, but the Lord delivers us from them all. He is a good, good Father, and He has not left us alone. You are not alone in this battle.

Even though we remain in these fragile human bodies, the angels do not. They are strong, powerful, and present. They are literally surrounding you. They are at your disposal, whether you see them or not; we have "Angelic Assistance in Spiritual Warfare."

Chapter 11

The Divine Counsel

The Divine Counsel of angelic beings is often overlooked by the casual readers of the Bible. However, it is unmistakably present in the pages of God's Word. You will be astonished by how powerful this counsel is in assisting God with what He allows to unfold on earth. This understanding will reveal greater insights than you have ever had before into the deep connection between heaven and earth.

Secret: There are ranks among the angels! Good or Bad!

As we delve deeper into angels in warfare, it becomes evident that there are ranks among the angelic forces. Without elaborating here, I'll simply name those found in The Word. They appear to be arranged in the following order:

Seraphim are those beings who continually proclaim the holiness of God, often referred to as the burning ones. They are depicted with hands and six wings.

Cherubim guard and take part in judgment. A cherub was stationed at the entrance of the Garden of Eden to prevent mankind from reentering. These angels differ in appearance; some have two faces, while others have four. They resemble humans and have four wings, with legs that appear calf-like. They move on wheels and support the throne of God.

The next rank consists of the Archangels. In the Book of Daniel, Michael the Archangel engages in spiritual warfare, battling against an evil prince. These angels are known as chief angels or princes.

On the flip side, there are evil princes. They appear to rule over worldly nations here on Earth. This is described as the ranking of the Kingdom of Darkness. The apostle Paul refers to them as principalities, evil rulers, and powers. While we don't have a clear biblical description of them or their specific duties, their titles give us a good sense of their assignments. *

Secret: There is a Divine Counsel in Heaven made up of angels!

There is another group of angels mentioned in the Word of God called the Divine Counsel. Many of you may not be familiar with this; perhaps you have never heard of them.

Why would God need or want a council? Many have never noticed this in the narrative; in fact, it took me a long time to pay attention to these passages. I had sought God for understanding about other passages that I had been contemplating. After asking God questions as I often do and waiting for Him to show me how the dots would connect, I was awakened from a deep sleep by a voice repeating, "Divine Counsel, Divine Counsel." This experience sent me on a journey to learn more. To me, it clarifies so much about how the supernatural realm operates. I hope it will be enlightening for you as well.

If you have a heart to explore more about the Divine Counsel, I recommend picking up a copy of Dr. Michael Heiser's book, "The Unseen Realm." It details the workings of God's Divine Counsel in depth. His book is thoroughly documented with proof texts for the concepts he presents. The Divine Counsel of God consists of angelic beings, and the following pages will demonstrate this clearly.

I don't plan to delve deeply into this reality, just to make you aware of its existence. You'll want to grasp its workings and how they manifest the will of God on Earth. You're going to be amazed at how active this counsel is in creating supernatural circumstances in the unseen realm.

* (1) Is.14:29, (2) Ez.1:10, 10:14, 41:18-19 (3) Eph.1:21,3:10, 6:12, Rm.8:38, Col.1:16,

They are highly effective in assisting God with His plans and in spiritual warfare.

God created two families. Before He restored the heavens and the earth and created humankind, He had already established His angelic family.

God's earthly family (you and me) is clearly visible to our human eyes. However, God's first family, known as the "Sons of God," His angelic force, remains invisible to us. It seems that not every angel loyal to the throne of God is part of this Divine Council. Other angels fulfill different duties and supernatural roles.

So, what is "The Divine Counsel"? Let's explore this through the text. Our first stop is the Book of Job. In this passage, God is engaging with Job to correct his false accusations against Him. I shared some of this at the beginning of this book. Now, we will go deeper.

> *"Where were you when I laid the foundation of the earth? Tell Me, if you know and have understanding." "Who determined the measurements [of the earth], if you know? Or who stretched the [measuring] line on it? "On what were its foundations fastened? Or who laid its cornerstone, when the **morning stars** sang together, and all the **angels** shouted for joy. Job. 38:4-7 Amp.*

In the scriptures, the term "star" often refers to angels (Strongs H3558). A star denotes the rank of a prince. As mentioned above, there are ranks of authority in the heavens, just as there are in the Kingdom of Darkness.

All the sons of God—the angels—shouted for joy. When humankind was created, the angels watched the Master complete His magnificent and incredible work. When He declared that His work was finished and that it was good, all the angels (sons of God) shouted for joy.

The word "sons" in Hebrew means exactly that: "sons," referring to a family and a builder of the family name. Therefore, when we discuss the "sons of God," we refer to the sons of a family that builds a family name.

> *Give unto the LORD, O ye mighty, give unto the LORD glory and strength. Ps. 29:1*

The phrase, "Oh, ye mighty," corresponds to the same number H1121 in The Strong's Concordance, which means "sons"—a name that signifies a family connection. The mighty are sons; they are beings related to the Father.

> *.....God standeth in the congregation of the mighty; he judgeth among the gods. Ps. 82:1*

How can he judge among the gods? I thought He was the only God. So, who are these other gods? The term "gods" in Hebrew refers to a superlative angel, a magistrate, or a judge. They are part of God's Divine Council. The use of the word "god" indicates an ordinary deity, not the supreme God. Our God is supreme and above all others. He is the Creator and Father. He judges the lesser gods, the angels of Ps. 82.

Secret: YHVH is the supreme God who judges other gods!

I could linger here by providing additional scriptures that support God's Divine Counsel. Nevertheless, a couple of stories make this concept abundantly clear. They reveal angelic assistance in warfare without question and illustrate how the Divine Counsel carries out God's will in the lives of mankind and the destiny of nations. A prime example of the Divine Counsel is found in 1 Kings.

To help you understand better what has led to this Angelic Counsel meeting, you'll need the background of these verses. It's important to see the complete picture of how God's sons are considered in His decisions. Not only do they offer Him suggestions on the need for judgment, but they also assist in executing those judgments. Our key verse here will be verse 20.

> *"'I will go and be a deceiving spirit in the mouths of all his prophets,' he said. "You will succeed in enticing him,' said the LORD. 'Go and do it.'* 1 Kings 22:20

Syria had conquered Israel, the northern kingdom ruled by King Ahab. However, the King of Syria permitted Israel to stay in their territory but imposed heavy taxes on them. In the third year of taxation, King Ahab strategized to wage war against Syria to reclaim its independence.

At the same time, Ahab and King Jehoshaphat of Judah, the southern kingdom, settled their differences after years of conflict. This led Ahab to seek Jehoshaphat's assistance in his fight against the Syrians.

When Ahab presented his plans to go to war, Jehoshaphat replied, "Have you inquired of YHVH (Yahweh)?" Ahab, a profoundly wicked king married to the notoriously evil Queen Jezebel, responded by gathering 400 of his false prophets of Baal. All 400 of these prophets boldly proclaimed with much fanfare that Ahab would be successful in battle and return victorious.

Secret: Liars stick together.

He loved what these prophets told him. One of them even tied together two bull horns and prophesied that Ahab would completely push back Syria just as a bull drives his horns into an opponent. Ahab envisioned himself riding back into Samaria with the masses cheering his success.

Jehoshaphat, who sought to follow the Torah and serve the God of Israel, did not trust these prophets and called for Micaiah to prophesy for Yahweh. Nowhere in the scriptures do we find Jehoshaphat asking God whether he should ally with Ahab or not.

What happened next infuriated Ahab, who already hated Micaiah. Initially, Micaiah agreed with the other prophets because he had been threatened not to speak anything different. However, Ahab suspected that Micaiah was lying and told him to speak only what God was genuinely saying. Micaiah then declared that all 400 of Ahab's prophets were liars. He informed Ahab that a **lying spirit sent from God** was in the mouths of all the other prophets. He foretold that he saw all of Israel scattered on the sides of the hill like sheep without a shepherd.

Think about that! A lying spirit sent from God! This was not what Ahab wanted to hear. His response was to imprison Micaiah while he went to battle against Syria. He was told he would stay there until Ahab returned victorious.

Ahab devised a plan to disguise himself but instructed Jehoshaphat to wear his royal garments into battle. (What a great friend!) These instructions made Jehoshaphat the main target of the Syrian army. Unbeknownst to Jehoshaphat, the King of Syria had ordered his soldiers to kill no one, whether great or small, but to focus solely on Ahab. Ahab's plan positioned Jehoshaphat as the only one in royal attire, and he was unaware of the danger he had put himself in.

Secret: Pay attention to the true character of a person who claims to be your friend!

Naturally, the Syrian army mistook Jehoshaphat for Ahab. In the heat of battle, Jehoshaphat found himself cornered. What a surprise! He quickly cried out to God.

By the sovereignty of God Almighty, the enemy realized he was not Ahab. They let him go free. As the battle rages on, an arrow is accidentally shot without a target in sight. Yet, it "just so happened" to strike Ahab in his disguise. It pierced his armor through a small opening, and he died right there on the battlefield. His chariot was driven back to Samaria with his lifeless body, and the dogs licked up his blood in the streets. There is no escaping the plan of the Almighty!

Now, let's read this together, starting with verse 18 of 1 Kings 22. We can see how everything unfolded in heaven with the Divine Council. You'll notice that there was a meeting in heaven to decide how Ahab was to be killed in battle. Verse 18 reveals how upset Ahab is with Micaiah.

> *And the king of Israel said unto Jehoshaphat, Did I not tell thee that he would prophesy no good concerning me, but evil? And he said, Hear thou therefore the word of the LORD: I saw the LORD sitting on his throne, and all the **host** of heaven standing by him on his right hand and on his left. And the LORD said, Who shall persuade Ahab, that he may go up and fall at Ramothgilead? And one said on this manner, and another said on that manner. 1 Ki. 22:18-20*

Micaiah reported seeing Yahweh on His Throne, surrounded by the Host of Heaven.

In the Hebrew language, the word "host" signifies a mass of people regularly organized for war—a term for an army or a campaign and for soldiers waiting for battle. The host surrounding the Throne consists of warriors prepared for conflict. These are God's Angel Armies. He is the General, "A Man of War." Yahweh is His name.

Who will persuade? In Hebrew, the word "paw-thaw" means, in a sinister way, to delude, to allure, to deceive, to entice, to flatter, or to persuade.

The phrase "Make to go" means to spring up or ascend suddenly; Ahab is filled with an urgency to go to war. He has been spiritually triggered to move quickly!

> *And there came forth a spirit, and stood before the LORD, and said, I will persuade him. And the LORD said unto him, Wherewith? And he said, I will go forth, and I will be a lying spirit in the mouth of all his prophets. And he said, Thou shalt persuade him, and prevail also: go forth, and do so. 1 Ki. 22:21-22*

The Divine Counsel makes decrees, and they execute what is written.

What! We have just seen God the Father meet with a council where they decide how to persuade Ahab to declare war and enter a battle where he would be killed. Did you know that these kinds of council meetings occur in the heavens? Did you know that God Himself can place a lying spirit in the mouth of a false prophet? It makes me wonder if this king was so evil that his time simply ran out, and it was his moment to die. His days were numbered. In reality, when Micaiah told him the truth, it was his last chance on this earth to repent. Instead, he responded in anger and persecuted God's prophet.

> *Now therefore, behold, the LORD hath put a lying spirit in the mouth of all these thy prophets, and the LORD hath spoken evil concerning thee. But Zedekiah the son of Chenaanah went near, and smote Micaiah on the cheek, and said, Which way went the Spirit of the LORD from me to speak unto thee? And Micaiah said, Behold, thou shalt see in that day, when thou shalt go into an inner chamber to hide thyself. 1 Kings 22:23-25*

> *And the king of Israel said, Take Micaiah, and carry him back unto Amon the governor of the city, and to Joash the king's son; And say, Thus saith the king, Put this fellow in the prison, and feed him with bread of affliction and with water of affliction, until I come in peace. And Micaiah said, If thou return at all in peace, the LORD hath not spoken by me. And he said, Hearken, O people, every one of you. So the king of Israel and Jehoshaphat the king of Judah went up to Ramothgilead. 1 Ki. 22:26-29*

Jehoshaphat was persuaded to go, despite the prophet of God advising against it. These are the kinds of situations we need to be cautious about. When we feel we shouldn't go, but the majority thinks otherwise, what will you do?

> *And the king of Israel said unto Jehoshaphat, I will disguise myself, and enter into the battle; but put thou on thy robes. And the king of Israel disguised himself and went into the battle. But the king of Syria commanded his thirty and two captains that had rule over his chariots, saying, Fight neither with small nor great, save only with the king of Israel. And it came to pass, when the captains of the chariots saw Jehoshaphat, that they said, Surely it is the king of Israel. And they turned aside to fight against him: and Jehoshaphat cried out. And it came to pass, when the captains of the chariots perceived that it was not the king of Israel, that they turned back from pursuing him And a certain man drew a bow at a venture, and smote the king of Israel between the joints of the harness: wherefore he said unto the driver of his chariot, Turn thine hand, and carry me out of the host; for I am wounded. And the battle increased that day: and the king was stayed up in his chariot against the Syrians, and died at even: and the blood ran out of the wound into the midst of the chariot. And there went a proclamation throughout the host about the going down of the sun, saying, Every man to his city, and every man to his own country. So the king died and was brought to Samaria; and they buried the king in Samaria. Samaria was the capital of Israel. And one washed the chariot in the pool of Samaria; and the dogs licked up his blood; and they washed his armour; according unto the word of the LORD which he spake. 1 Ki. 22;30-38*

The dogs' licking up the blood of Ahab in the streets was prophesied by Elijah in 1 Kings 21:17

Let's review this once more. In verse 22 of this chapter, it states:

> *And the LORD said unto him, wherewith? And he said, I will go forth, and I will be a **lying spirit** in the mouth of all his prophets.*

> *And He said, Thou shalt persuade him, and prevail also: go forth, and do so. 1 Kings 22:22*

Four hundred prophets of Baal spoke with one voice. However, when Micaiah was called to represent Yahweh, he told Ahab that a lying spirit from Yahweh was in the mouths of his prophets. He was speaking the truth to Ahab, but Ahab chose to believe a lie.

God was speaking to His counsel, asking who would persuade Ahab to go to battle. One offered a suggestion, while another had a different idea. This is God's counsel; they are not instructing God but brainstorming, so to speak. Each provided input for the best solution, making suggestions as requested. God sought their insights. In this vision, God sits on His throne, surrounded by His council members. This is what the true prophet of God, Micaiah saw in the spirit.

Ahab heard **words**. He chose to believe a false, deceitful **word**, leading him to his death. Those words were sent from God to bring about his destruction. A supernatural influence is at work in this story. We learned earlier how important "words" are. What we choose to believe, is a life and death matter!

Jehoshaphat, dressed in royal robes, cried out. Was it an angel who turned the chariots around, causing the Syrians to stop pursuing him? Was it an angel who guided the arrow to strike precisely the right spot to wound Ahab? It was shot by accident, according to the Word. It is decreed by God Himself that Ahab must die, even if he is disguised.

If you heard 400 so-called prophets saying the same thing, who would you trust? Could you rely on what you heard directly from the Spirit of God instead?

This story is recounted in 2 Chronicles 18, which provides a bit more detail. Once again, he said:

> *Therefore hear the word of the LORD; I saw the LORD sitting upon his throne, and all the host of heaven standing on his right hand and on his left. 2 Chron. 18:18*

Micaiah clearly declares this to be the "Word of the Lord!" The host of heaven is an angelic army that chooses to send a lying spirit. This is God's army surrounding Him. They are gathered to receive orders from Headquarters. Together, they make a final decision about the fate of King Ahab. These angelic beings united as a council and formulated a plan.

Remember, the hosts of heaven (Strongs H6635) are a multitude of beings, organized for war, **an army**. It is a campaign of worshippers there for an appointed time. They are an **army** ready for battle. They are soldiers waiting upon war.

This is a council surrounding the Throne of God, and they are waiting for a war. When the final war on earth is determined, they will have centuries of experience. They devised a sinister plan to lure Ahab to his death. Listen, this was an incredibly wicked man. It was time for his evil reign to end. We will see the same thing happen in America. A day will come when judgment will be made to put an end to wickedness.

Ahab felt an urgency to go to war. He's in a hurry. He desires to engage in battle. His eagerness leads him to accept the lies of the prophets. What will the last days be like? It appears that even now, nations are eager for conflict. Is this why Jesus warned us not to be deceived? What spirit lies behind the words we hear? The orders for Ahab's destruction had been issued.

This is the same account found in the Amplified Bible, as documented in 2 Chronicles 18. It provides additional details.

> *Now Jehoshaphat had great wealth and honor, and was allied by marriage with Ahab. Some years later he went down to [visit] Ahab in Samaria. And Ahab slaughtered many sheep and oxen for him and the people who were with him, and **induced** him to*

go up against Ramoth-gilead. Ahab king of Israel said to Jehoshaphat king of Judah, "Will you go with me to [fight against] Ramoth-gilead?" He answered, "I am as you are, and my people as your people [your hopes and concerns are ours]; we will be with you in the battle."

Further, Jehoshaphat said to the king of Israel, "Please inquire first for the word of the LORD." Then the king of Israel assembled the prophets, four hundred men, and said to them, "Shall we go against Ramoth-gilead to battle, or shall I refrain?" And they said, "Go up, for God will hand it over to the king." But Jehoshaphat said, "Is there no prophet of the LORD still here by whom we may inquire?" The king of Israel said to Jehoshaphat, "There is still one man by whom we may inquire of the LORD, but I hate him, for he never prophesies [anything] good for me, but always evil. He is Micaiah the son of Imla" And Jehoshaphat said, "Let not the king say so [perhaps this time it will be different]." 2 Chron. 18:1-7

Ahab's False Prophets Assure Victory

Then the king of Israel called for an officer and said, "Bring Micaiah the son of Imla quickly." Now the king of Israel and Jehoshaphat the king of Judah were sitting, each on his throne, arrayed in their robes; they were sitting at the threshing floor at the entrance of the gate of Samaria; and all the prophets were prophesying before them. Zedekiah the son of Chenaanah had made horns of iron for himself; and said, "Thus says the LORD: 'With these you shall gore the Arameans (Syrians) until they are destroyed.' All the prophets prophesied this, saying, "Go up to Ramoth-gilead and succeed; the LORD will hand it over to the king."

Micaiah Brings the true Word from God

The messenger who went to call Micaiah said to him, "Listen, the words of the prophets are of one accord, foretelling a favorable outcome for the king. So just let your word be like one of them and speak favorably." But Micaiah said, "As the LORD lives, I will [only] speak what my God says."

When he came to the king, the king said to him, "Micaiah, shall we go to Ramoth-gilead to battle, or shall I refrain?" And he said, "Go up and succeed, for they will be handed over to you." Then the king said to him, "How many times must I warn you (make you swear an oath) to tell me nothing but the truth in the name of the LORD?" Then Micaiah said, "I saw all [the people of] Israel Scattered on the mountains, As sheep that have no shepherd; And the LORD said, 'These have no master. Let each one return to his house in peace.'" Then the king of Israel said to Jehoshaphat, "Did I not tell you that he would not prophesy good in regard to me, but [only] evil?"

*So Micaiah said, "Therefore, hear the word of the LORD: I saw the LORD sitting on His throne, and all the host **(army) of heaven** standing on His right and on His left. Then the LORD said, 'Who will entice Ahab king of Israel to go up and fall [defeated] at Ramoth-gilead?' And one said this, and another said that. Then a spirit came forward and stood before the LORD and said, 'I will entice him.' The LORD said to him, 'By what means?' He said, 'I will go out and be a **deceptive spirit** in the mouth of all his prophets.' Then the LORD said, 'You are to entice him and also succeed. Go and do so.' Now, you see, the LORD put a deceptive spirit in the mouth of these prophets of yours; and the LORD has [actually] proclaimed disaster against you." Then Zedekiah the son of Chenaanah came up and struck Micaiah on the cheek and said, "Which way did the Spirit of the LORD go [when he departed] from me to speak to you?" Micaiah said, "Behold, you will see on that day when you go into an inner*

> *room [desperately trying] to hide yourself." Then the king of Israel said, "Take Micaiah and return him to Amon the governor of the city and to Joash the king's son, and say, 'Thus says the king: "Put this man in prison and feed him just enough bread and water to survive until I return in peace (safely)." But Micaiah said, "If you actually return in peace, the LORD has not spoken by me." And he added, "Listen [to what I have said], you people, all of you."*

The reaction of the false prophet mirrors that of today's politicians. When they are exposed, they become furious and shift the blame onto the person who has revealed their deception. Consider that even Jehoshaphat was swayed by the false prophets. He chose to align himself with Ahab instead of heeding the warning of the Lord!

Ahab's Defeat and Death

> *So [Ahab] the king of Israel and Jehoshaphat king of Judah went up against Ramoth-gilead. The king of Israel said to Jehoshaphat, "I will disguise myself and will go into battle, but you put on your [royal] robes." So the king of Israel disguised himself, and they went into the battle. Now the king of Aram (Syria) had commanded the captains of his chariots, saying, "Do not fight with the small or the great, but only with the king of Israel." So when the captains of the chariots saw Jehoshaphat [of Judah], they said, "It is the king of Israel!" So they turned to fight against him, but **Jehoshaphat called out [for God's help], and the LORD helped him**; and God diverted them away from him. When the captains of the chariots saw that it was not the king of Israel, they turned back from pursuing him. Then a certain man drew his bow at random and struck [Ahab] the king of Israel between the scales of his armor. So Ahab said to his chariot driver, "Turn around and take me out of the battle, because I am seriously wounded." The battle raged that day, and the king of*

Israel propped himself up in his chariot in front of the Arameans (Syrians) until the evening, and at sunset he died. 2 Chron. 18:8-34

We have more detail here in the 2 Chronicles' account of this battle. In verse 31, Jehoshaphat cried out to the Lord, and the Lord helped him and delivered him from the enemy. God, Elohim, moved them to depart from him.

So, now we know why the Syrians didn't kill Jehoshaphat. This king serves Yahweh and knows where his help comes from. He cried out to the Lord. He was in the heat of battle, and his immediate response was, "Yahweh, HELP ME!" He cried out to the Lord, and the Lord helped him.

The phrase "Helped him" is H5826 in the Strongs. **It means he became surrounded** and protected; it means to **assist** and support in times of hardship and distress.

Who do you think he got surrounded by? God moved the enemy to depart from him.

The word "God" is Elohim. It refers to a superlative angel. Superlative is of the highest quality or degree. Highest, or bravest, most fierce, someone embodying excellence. These are angels that have come to the aide of Jehoshaphat and forced the Syrians to retreat. (Strongs H430)

Then. In 2 Ch 18:33 a man drew a bow by a venture. Venture is risk, gambling. Like speculation, chance. In other words, it is a long shot. (Strongs H8537) and it just happens to enter between the scales of Ahab's armor. I am sure you have seen this kind of armor that is rows of scales. How did an arrow enter Ahab's armor between the scales? What are the odds of that happening?

God sent angels during a fierce and raging earthly battle. Let me express that differently. Just as the angels fought alongside Joshua in Jericho, they were present in the battle with Jehoshaphat. How did the enemy's chariots get turned around? Perhaps it was like King David when he prayed for the angels to chase his enemies.

Then, in some mysterious way, an arrow that wasn't even intended to be shot was perfectly guided to deliver the death blow to King Ahab. This arrow was a gamble, a long shot. No one ever gets any credit for the kill. The one who managed to slay King Ahab should have at least received a mention, yet there is never any recognition for it. It struck precisely where the joints of Ahab's armor met, ensuring his demise. It reminded me of how David threw the stone at Goliath, hitting him in exactly the right spot to bring a giant to the ground. Do you suspect that any of this might have involved angelic direction? We don't know that David didn't have angelic assistance for that stone to hit in the exact place it needed to. This arrow was sent to the precise location it was meant to go. Even with armor on, Ahab could not escape the decree of the Divine Council.

Secret: This Divine Counsel from heaven directly interacts with humans on earth.

God's power is not about how skilled of a marksman anyone is. It doesn't rely on our greatness in the natural world. Instead, it's about how great our God is and what He does in and for us, even in the midst of war. In the chaos and confusion of battle, He sends His angels to turn the enemy around and to save our lives. He provides angelic assistance to those of us who are serving Him. We are in this war together.

> *I will go and be a deceiving spirit in the mouths of all his prophets,' he said. "'You will succeed in enticing him,' said the LORD. 'Go and do it.' NIV 2 Chron. 18:21.*

It was determined and destined by the divine counsel of God that Ahab was going to die on that day. And that is exactly what happened.

This was not the only time in the Bible when an evil spirit was sent from heaven. It also happened to King Saul. It makes me wonder if this kind of judgment is reserved solely for those in power over nations. Of course, that's strictly speculation. The Book of First Samuel doesn't provide details about the Divine Council's role in King Saul's situation. However, the patterns certainly appear similar. Saul had been rebellious towards the Lord's instructions, resulting in his kingdom being stripped from him.

> *But now thy kingdom shall not continue: the LORD hath sought him a man after his own heart, and the LORD hath commanded him to be captain over his people, because thou hast not kept that which the LORD commanded thee. 1 Sam. 13:14 NLT*

God saw Saul's rebellion to be a form of witchcraft, and he was judged for it.

> *Rebellion is as sinful as witchcraft, and stubbornness as bad as worshiping idols. So, because you have rejected the command of the LORD, he has rejected you as king." 1 Sam.15:23 NLT*

> *Now the Spirit of the LORD had departed from Saul, and **an evil spirit from the LORD tormented** him. 1 Sam. 16:14 NLT*

Secret: It is possible for an evil spirit to be sent from God.

God is sovereign. He knows the end from the beginning. That spirit of rebellion in Saul would ultimately lead the entire nation to follow him in his rebellion against Yahweh. God had an eternal plan: to send a redeemer King who would establish a Kingdom that would never end. The promise of the Messiah would be given to King David, a man after God's own heart, and not to Saul.

Those of us in a relationship with Jesus/Yeshua (sons and daughters) understand that if an evil spirit tries to attack us, we invoke the "blood of the Lamb" and His finished work on Calvary that paid for all our transgressions. Because our lives are hidden with Christ in God, we are already dead to this world and alive in Christ Jesus.

> *For ye are dead, and your life is hid with Christ in God. Col. 3:3*

As a very young woman, I lived outside of God's will for a short time. Because God could see the end from the beginning, He spared me more times than I can remember. Looking back at that season in my life, I should have died. Instead, God continued to place His angels around me to protect me.

One event stands out in my memory. I was 21 years old and on my way to a job interview in downtown St. Louis. I was driving a little green Maverick sporty car when I entered an intersection with a green arrow signaling me to go. I never saw what was coming. Another vehicle failed to notice the red light and crashed full force into the passenger side of my car.

Secret: God knows the end from the beginning in your life

The impact was so powerful that it spun my car around. Before everything stopped spinning, my vehicle had been smashed in on three sides. I was not serving God at that time, but I knew Him. As soon as I felt the impact, I screamed, "Jesus Christ." I didn't know to call on the Lord; I had never even heard of doing such a thing. It was more like an expression. I had grown up hearing my dad use that expression to reflect his disgust or surprise. It wasn't a prayer; it was just an expression.

I had no understanding of calling on God's name. In preparation for writing this book, The Father had me relive those moments of that accident. My car was completely totaled; it looked as if it had been hit by a wrecking ball on three sides. Yet, I walked away with just scrapes on my shins. I can still see in my memory the green arrow signaling me to go that day. I could almost hear the sound of metal clanging all around me as my car spun uncontrollably in circles. As I reflected on that moment, the Lord said to me, "I heard you. You called out My name. In a crisis, you called My name; that's what came out of your mouth, and the angels heard it!"

I am absolutely convinced that somehow the angels guided how that car hit me to prevent any lifelong physical injury. There's no other explanation for why I wasn't taken away in an ambulance. Instead, just like Jehoshaphat in battle, I was surrounded by angels.

As I type this, I am moved to tears by the goodness of God. My heart cries out in gratitude and worship for His saving grace. The scriptures say, "He who calls on the name of the Lord shall be saved." Even when I was ignorant and rebellious, I called on His name, and He saved me. He looked down through the corridors of time and knew that one day I would be proclaiming His righteous acts to the world. He knew the end from the beginning.

I am so glad that at that moment I called out His name. I lived among people who took God's name in vain. I often heard the expression G.D., but that's not what came out of my mouth. I yelled for Jesus, and I will continue to do so for the rest of my life. Now, I know who I am in Christ Jesus. I know that He lives in me and that I walk in His incredible power. As I have grown in the Lord and committed to being more like Him daily, He has entrusted me with greater truths continually and has allowed me to even enter heavenly places with Him. As we behold Him, we become like Him. He is the epitome of selfless love.

Recently, I saw angels with wings, something I hadn't witnessed before. All the angels I had seen previously had no wings.

I saw The Ancient of Days. He stood surrounded by many angelic beings. He spoke to me from their midst and said, "Sharon, as you read My Word, you observe countless angelic beings." He was addressing my questions about the Divine Counsel.

I had asked, "Why does God need advice?" His response to me was, "No one is advising me. Everything here is done in order. Only one of those in the council speaks at a time. Just as Paul taught, everything is decent and in order. "Oh," he continued with a smile, "I already know what I will do. I lovingly consider the suggestions of the members of My Divine Council, the family. They are eager to serve Me earnestly. I allow them to be part of My judgments. Then I either accept or disallow their input."

> *Do you not know that we will judge angels? How much more the things that pertain to this life? 1Cor. 6:3*

Secret: You will judge angels!

That resolved my wondering issues. Consider this: "We will judge angels." We will be a kingdom of priests, and we will judge angels. That's what He is doing with His other family (the Divine Council) right now. They already possess glorified eternal bodies.

I asked the Lord if the 400 prophets were aware they had lying spirits. He replied, "It only takes one to lie, and the others will follow. It's in their nature!" This is how deception operates: it influences by compelling people to agree or disagree. People are used to spreading lies, and they can even influence kings. They go to war based on falsehoods. Even if they are orchestrating their own death."

Are we missing the intervention of the Divine Counsel? How did the arrow strike Ahab in exactly the right spot to ensure his death? How did the stone that struck Goliath in the head, bringing him immediately to his knees, hit him in the precise spot to render him unconscious? Are we missing the activity of angelic assistance? Are we to understand angelic assistance without it being spelled out for us?

These two chapters make clear the workings of the Divine Counsel. Can we take this information and apply it to other places in the scripture? I think we are supposed to.

> *It is the glory of God to conceal a thing: but the honour of kings is to search out a matter. Pr. 25:2*

This was what motivated me to learn about the Divine Counsel. A dispute arose over a sermon that another sister was promoting. In this sermon, the preacher stated that Satan sits at the table with Jesus every day, eating and having conversations. I immediately rejected that idea. The thought of Jesus and Satan having lunch and discussing individuals was troubling! Jesus came to destroy the works of the Devil, not to be friendly with him. This sister dismissed all Biblical reasoning. So, I began seeking the Lord for a definitive answer. That's when the phrase "Divine Counsel" stirred me awake in the middle of the night.

After searching the scriptures on this matter, I conclude that if Satan speaks to God daily, it is only in the "Courtroom of Heaven," where he accuses the brethren day and night.

> *And I heard a loud voice saying in heaven, Now is come salvation, and strength, and the kingdom of our God, and the power of his Christ: for the **accuser of our brethren** is cast down, which **accused them** before our God day and night. Rev. 12:10*

God has His Divine Counsel, and Satan is not part of that counsel!

It's wonderful to consider how God includes His angelic family in His divine strategies. The Word reminds us that we will have the privilege to judge angels and guide the nations. We can be thankful that we always have angelic company on this journey. Hopefully, we are all cultivating a closer relationship with, and a deeper appreciation for, the angels who come to our aid. Often, we don't even realize we're reaching out for help. Lord, open our spiritual eyes to see and our ears to hear what the Spirit is sharing with the Body of Messiah here on earth. Keep your eyes constantly on Jesus, and you will remain vigilant against the lies of the enemy.

Don't listen to the masses and be easily persuaded by the crowd. It's okay to say, "No, I don't feel led to do that," regardless of the immediate consequences from man.

> *The LORD is with me; I will not be afraid. What can mere mortals do to me? Ps. 118:6 NIV*

Thank you for allowing me to share this with you. I find it extremely powerful information.

For further studies on the topic in detail: Michael Hieser, The Unseen Realm, Lexhan Press 2015.

Chapter 12

The Decree of The Watchers!

Spiritual warfare encompasses our prayer time, the actions we take during prayer, and the way we pray. It demonstrates how aggressive and assertive we are on the front lines of battle. This can vary based on the level of anointing and passion we hold for the issues we pray about.

Is there a difference between spiritual warfare and prayer? When we engage in warfare, we confront the enemy. In contrast, when we pray, we address King Jesus/Yeshua. At times, our prayers may shift into warfare, making it difficult to determine where one ends and the other begins. The important thing is that we engage on both levels.

In both prayer and warfare, we make declarations, emphatically proclaiming what the Word of God has already established through what is written. We are speaking God's Word into the world. In prayer, we honor, adore, and worship God, proclaiming who He is and His great power. We make our petitions known to Him.

> *And this is the confidence that we have in him, that, if we ask anything according to his will, he heareth us: And if we know that he hear us, whatsoever we ask, we know that we have the petitions that we desired of him. 1 Jn 5:14-15*

When we enter into warfare mode; we declare the demise of the enemy and the wicked according to the Word of God. We announce to principalities the purposes and final decrees of our God concerning His people and the earth. We proclaim our authority on the earth secured by the suffering, death, burial, and resurrection of our Lord Jesus! He has triumphed over death and the grave.

> *I am he that liveth, and was dead; and, behold, I am alive for evermore, Amen; and have the keys of hell and of death. Rv. 1:18*

When we consider war in the physical realm, we recognize that various roles and positions must be filled. Each requires specific qualifications in knowledge, skills, or talents. Some individuals serve as supportive staff, while others are on the front lines or in the trenches.

Others are fighting from the air. Reconnaissance, planning, and various activities are essential in warfare. The Kingdom of Heaven operates similarly. Therefore, what we need to understand is what God has specifically called us to do.

What I have discovered is that when we gather as a group to pray or when we engage in spiritual warfare, that's usually when we notice an angelic presence—either during or right after our intense prayer. There is increased spiritual power in numbers!

Locally, we meet as a group to pray weekly. Many of us feel or sense this angelic presence; there's just a knowing that we are not alone. On occasion, the angels will manifest or reveal themselves in one way or the other. Several of us have witnessed the demonstration of an angelic presence among us. We have seen them come in response to our obedience and our willingness to pray.

Single angels have appeared more often. Groups of angels seem to be rarer. They were observed lined up at the back of the property, prepared for battle. As we engage in spiritual combat, they remain ready to fight alongside us. It's as if they are waiting for our prayers to trigger their commands to act from heaven—almost as if they are anticipating the breaking of the heavenly seals.

In the last chapter, we witnessed King Ahab's death and the angels' role in orchestrating his demise. In this chapter, we'll investigate the decree of the angels (watchers) concerning Nebuchadnezzar, King of Babylon.

We know from the scriptures that angels participated in rescuing King Jehoshaphat, who was caught in the wrong place at the wrong time. A plan was initiated in the heavenly realm by the angels with God's consent to execute their plan here on Earth. God didn't make these decisions alone. While He doesn't require anyone to advise or counsel Him, He chooses to involve His family of angelic beings in His planning sessions. He permitted them to suggest ways to achieve a desired outcome in matters on Earth.

Secret: The demise of an evil ruler is settled in Heaven before it manifests on Earth!

When it came to determining how Ahab's life would end, there were several suggestions from God's divine counsel, with one considered the best solution.

We're not told how many prayers may have ascended, pleading with God to remove Ahab from power. However, there is a pattern in the Scriptures that suggests that someone was praying. Throughout our lives, we see evil leaders around the globe; as praying Christians, we carry a responsibility to challenge their actions through prayer. It's crucial that we are not misled by media reports. The Scriptures tell us that we can train our senses to discern good from evil.

> *But strong meat belongeth to them that are of full age, even those who by reason of use have their senses exercised to discern both good and evil. Heb. 5:14*

We must exercise discernment to know whom to listen to and whom not to. Each day, we encounter information presented as news in the media, but for many of us, it's merely old information and not news at all. This is because we have chosen not to believe the lies previously promoted by the same media.

Take heed therefore how ye hear.....Luke 8:18

They present their newscast as if they have just discovered a current truth. It's not exactly news; it's the disclosure of information that was previously concealed from the public. It's all about their scheduled timing to best control the masses. What they eventually share is stale and outdated information- not news at all!

For God's people who sought truth at the beginning of the plandemic, they uncovered facts years before the public was informed. They refused to accept the narrative put forth by the mainstream media. Even as great evidence comes forth exposing lies, many continue to choose to hold on to the original stories told. It is difficult for them to admit that they might have been wrong about anything at all.

In Ahab's situation, he chose to believe all the lying prophets. That made it easier for him to unjustly imprison the only person telling him the truth. It ultimately cost Ahab his life.

Secret: Believing the nightly news could cost you your life!

None of us are promised tomorrow. We learn more each day about the wickedness of the earth and evil plans to destroy humankind if possible. At times, we wonder, why doesn't God judge this? Where is righteousness? Where is justice?

Is there more that we, as God's army on earth, can do? Instead of wondering why God doesn't remove many of the wicked, perhaps we need to pray in a more focused way for evil to be destroyed and for justice to prevail.

It's easy to get caught up in reading articles, listening to sermons, and researching rather than engaging in spiritual warfare. The devil will do whatever he can to keep you occupied with anything but battling him in the spirit. When we pray, we create an impact.

Sometimes, Christians resemble soldiers on R & R — rest and relaxation. We are not supposed to be resting when everything is falling apart around the world. God is seeking someone to stand in the gap. We are required to remain in the heat of the battle. God is always doing His part. He never slumbers or sleeps. He sees everything and misses nothing.

> *The eyes of the LORD are toward the righteous [those with moral courage and spiritual integrity] And His ears are open to their cry. Ps. 34:15 Amp.*

He is watching you. Hopefully, we have moral courage and spiritual integrity. When you cry out to the Lord, He hears you. Often, we aren't crying out to the Lord; we merely send up a " little dab will do ya" kind of prayer. Perhaps too many have a mindset that everything is already predetermined, so why pray? We aren't meant to simply watch things unfold before us. We are called to be in the midst of the battle until the end. Regardless of what seems to be predetermined by the Word, we still have a role to play in the final outcome.

> *The face of the LORD is against those who do evil, To cut off the memory of them from the earth. When the righteous cry [for help], the LORD hears And rescues them from all their distress and troubles. Ps. 34:16-17*

Our prayer is to be a cry. Are we that desperate? When we are, God rescues us from all our distress and all our troubles. Sometimes, we don't cry loud enough or long enough. We ask once and then lack the stamina or fortitude to persist. The Word tells us that when we start knocking, we should keep knocking. Continue praying or thanking Him for the answer until it manifests.

> *The LORD is near to the heartbroken And He saves those who are crushed in spirit (contrite in heart, truly sorry for their sin). (True repentance) Ps. 34:18*

When He speaks of the brokenhearted, He is referring to the humble—people with truly repentant hearts. Those are the individuals to whom he is closest.

> *Many hardships and perplexing circumstances confront the righteous, But the LORD rescues him from them all. Ps. 34:19*

When you face hardships, is it due to righteousness? Is the enemy against you? Does he stand opposed to you? You have the strength to fight back. Don't lie down and accept what he brings. If he delivers an unwanted package of sickness, misery, or trouble to your doorstep, tell the devil he has the wrong address, the wrong house—"I'm not accepting it. That stuff isn't coming here!" Send it back to the one who sent it in the first place. Reverse the curse! Reverse the curse and send it back to where it came from. We are redeemed by the blood of the Lamb and don't have to accept the lies of the devil!

Secret: You can reverse the curse!

Your salvation comes from one source, Yeshua/Jesus, and when you spend time with Him it is obvious to others.

> *Now when the men of the Sanhedrin (Jewish High Court) saw the **confidence** and **boldness** of Peter and John, and grasped the fact that they were uneducated and untrained [ordinary] men, they were astounded, and began to recognize that they had been with Jesus. Act. 4:13*

People will recognize if you've been intimate with Yeshua. If you've been in His presence, others will notice it. We are to dwell in His presence so deeply that His glory overflows to everyone around us. The result will be that you speak with boldness and confidence!

Satan may be the god of this world, but the earth is the Lord's, along with its fullness and everything within it. Satan might govern the authorities of this world, but the earth itself still belongs to Yahweh. As the creator, He is the rightful owner! The devil claims to possess this earth, but he is gravely mistaken. God is our keeper.

> *He will not allow your foot to slip; He who **keeps** you will not slumber. Behold, He who keeps Israel Will neither slumber [briefly] nor sleep [soundly]. Ps. 121:3-4*

You, who are grafted into the family of Abraham through belief in Yeshua/Jesus, are one with Israel! God is the hope of Israel. He is our hope!

> *The LORD shall preserve thee from all evil: he shall **preserve thy soul**. The LORD shall preserve thy going out and thy coming in from this time forth, and even for evermore. Ps. 121-8*

Don't forget this! He is your protector from ALL evil. He is the keeper of your soul! He is the lover of your soul! Stop trying to protect yourselves; we must trust Him to safeguard us. Our flesh may die, but we continue to live; we just change addresses. The body is merely a garage for keeping the Ferrari or your Mercedes protected. What is truly valuable to God is housed within our hearts. Even if this body disintegrates and turns to dust, our spirit and soul will live forever with God.

While we are still in these bodies, we have the promise of Deuteronomy 28, which tells us that we are blessed going in and blessed going out. No matter what we are doing, we are being blessed.

> *"FOR THE EYES OF THE LORD ARE [looking favorably] UPON THE RIGHTEOUS (the upright), AND HIS EARS ARE ATTENTIVE TO THEIR PRAYER (eager to answer), BUT THE FACE OF THE LORD IS AGAINST THOSE WHO PRACTICE EVIL." 2 Pe. 3:12*

When you pray, remember that as righteous individuals striving to follow the commandments, living for God, loving Him, and trying to walk in His footsteps as His disciples, He is eager to answer you. He is attentive to your prayers. God is eager to answer you and is waiting for you to talk to Him. He is not on vacation. Even when you think answers are delayed, He has a reason.

> *The Lord does not delay [as though He were unable to act] and is not slow about His promise, as some count slowness, but is [extraordinarily] patient toward you, not wishing for any to perish but for all to come to repentance. 2 Pe 3:9*

If mankind believes that God does not act because He is unable, he is sadly mistaken. He demonstrates patience toward all of humanity. This is why we don't see people being struck down the moment they speak blasphemously about God. In the Book of Daniel, we will observe how patient God was with Nebuchadnezzar. Again, we will see the angels and their role in dealing with a powerful earthly king.

King Nebuchadnezzar had a dream, and Daniel interpreted it. The dream serves as a warning, and the King has been given time to repent. A similar situation is occurring with leadership around the world today; God is granting them time to repent. However, that time is rapidly running out!

When we examine the Prophet Daniel's heartfelt appeal to the king, the king has sinned. The poor have been treated unjustly, and desperate cries for justice have risen from the vulnerable. Many of these captives are from Israel, enduring hardships under this king. Some of them remember that God remains their source of strength. They recall the comforting words in the Psalms, trusting wholeheartedly that Yahweh is their one true hope. The focus verse in this fourth chapter of Daniel is verse 27.

> *Therefore, O king, let my advice to you be [considered and found] acceptable; break away now from your sins and exhibit your repentance by doing what is right, and from your wickedness by*

> *showing mercy to the poor, so that [if you repent] there may possibly be a continuance of your prosperity and tranquility and a healing of your error.' Dan. 4:27*

Daniel advises the King to break free from his sin. Therefore, this king has been given a chance to repent and has even been informed of what is required to demonstrate signs of repentance.

Many nations have leaders and politicians partaking in immoral actions. They remain unjudged as God continues to grant them time to repent. When people err and seek forgiveness, they must take steps to amend their wrongs. Regrettably, many refuse to repent. They opt to lie, cheat, and deny responsibility, failing to make any effort to make things right. Politicians seldom say, "I've truly messed up. I did the wrong thing." As followers of God, we must be ready to admit our sins and wrongdoings to rectify the harm we may have caused.

As we witness evil in our own nation, we, as believers, must pause and wait upon the Lord. He **will** act, but it will be in His own time. Our role is to continue praying and to cooperate with the **angels** as God dispatches them to assist us in our prayers and in our warfare.

> *But they that wait upon the Lord shall renew their strength; they shall mount up with wings as eagles; they shall run, and not be weary; and they shall walk, and not faint. Is. 40:31*

We can't faint or become weary in doing good. We must understand that justice will come for the wicked. We are to strive for the same kind of patience that God shows when He gives people space for repentance.

> *And let us not be weary in well doing: for in due season we shall reap, if we faint not. Gal. 6:9*

So, let's read this portion of scripture from the beginning and see how God sent angelic assistance in response to the prayers of His people. Prayer is one aspect of warfare. Your prayers make a difference. They are heard on high, and God and the angels respond.

> *"I, Nebuchadnezzar, was at rest in my house and prospering in my palace.* Dan. 4:4

He is not in poverty; he is prosperous. He states, "I was in my house, thriving in my palace." All his needs were met, just like those of the elite in today's world. They remain oblivious to the cries of the poor.

> *I saw a dream and it made me afraid; and the fantasies and thoughts and the visions [that appeared] in my mind as I lay on my bed kept alarming me.* Dan. 4:5 Amp.

Secret: The elite can be easily terrified, it only takes one dream from God!

He keeps experiencing this dream repeatedly, and he's growing increasingly fearful as time passes.

> *So I gave orders to bring in before me all the wise men of Babylon, so that they might make known to me the interpretation of the dream. Then the magicians, the enchanters (Magi), the Chaldeans [who were the master astrologers] and the diviners came in, and I told them the dream, but they could not interpret it and make known its meaning to me. But at last Daniel came in before me, whose name is Belteshazzar, after the name of my god, and in whom is a spirit of the holy gods; and I told the dream to him, saying,* Dan. 4:6-8

He has given Daniel the name of his own god, Belteshazzar. However, he realizes that there is a different, more powerful God that resides within Daniel.

The term "God" in Hebrew is "el-aw." It can refer to gods, magistrates, or a supreme angel. What Nebuchadnezzar sees in Daniel is the supernatural God (YHVH) who created heaven and earth. Now, he is going to flatter

Daniel a great deal. Saying that he knows nothing will certainly confuse him. This man is desperate for an answer.

> *'O Belteshazzar, chief of the magicians, because I know that a spirit of the holy gods is in you and no mystery baffles or troubles you, tell me the visions of my dream which I have seen, along with its interpretation. 'The visions that passed through my mind as I lay on my bed were these: I was looking, and behold, there was a in the middle of the earth, and its height was great. 'The tree grew large and became strong And its height reached to heaven, And it was visible to the end of the earth. Dan. 4:9-11*

So the tree can be seen everywhere.

> *'Its leaves were beautiful and its fruit abundant, And in it was food for all. The beasts of the field found shade under it, And the birds of the sky nested in its branches, And all living creatures fed themselves from it. Dan. 4:12*

The KJV says: and all flesh was fed of it.

bes-ar' in the Hebrew is mankind. So, this tree meets the needs of all mankind.

> *'And behold, I saw in the visions of my mind as I lay on my bed, an **angelic watcher**, a holy one, descended from heaven. Dan. 4:13*

Here, we notice how different angles come into play in a situation on Earth that truly deserves our attention. The people in Nebuchadnezzar's kingdom have been seeking justice. The ruler has not shown kindness to the vulnerable, leaving their needs unaddressed. They are reaching out to God for help.

> *'He shouted aloud and said this: "Cut down the tree and cut off its branches; Shake off its leaves and scatter its fruit; Let the*

> *living creatures run from under it And the birds fly from its branches. Dan. 4:14*

The phrase "Shouted aloud" in the Hebrew language has a deeper meaning of an army or strength, a truly **mighty army,** power. The angel in this dream has given a shout! A battle cry! This watcher is not just a single angel. God has sent an army.

> *"Nevertheless leave the stump with its roots in the ground, Bound with a band of iron and bronze In the new grass of the field; And let him be wet with the dew of heaven, And let him feed with the animals in the grass of the earth. Dan. 4:15*

Secret: God sends angels to deal with National leaders! More often than we realize.

To "feed" means this is his portion or this is what he **deserves**. He is going to start eating grass with the wild beasts. The word "bound" is (Strong's H613); in Hebrew, it means imprisonment. It implies that he will be tied to something or imprisoned in an encasing while he eats. Perhaps he will be in a stall somewhere with wild or domestic beasts. It doesn't tell us clearly.

> *"Let his mind and nature be changed from a man's And let an animal's mind and nature be given to him, And let seven periods of time pass over him. Dan. 4:16*

"Let his mind be changed" is to be altered and diverse. He loses his intellect and his ability to speak. He loses his ability to think clearly or to reason. The idea of this should be utterly terrifying. But for some reason, he doesn't take it seriously.

Recently, some people seem to have experienced a shift in their ability to think clearly. Something has happened to them. Their reasoning skills are impaired. Events are unfolding in various places around the world. There are many opinions about what this might be, but we are witnessing individuals who do not think rationally. They regard things that are factual by nature's standards (like gender) yet still insist that it is not true.

This sentence is by the decree of the angelic watchers. A decree has gone out and a decree has been made by the **angelic watchers**. This is the Divine counsel of God. The decision is a command of the holy ones. The Holy ones are the superior angelic beings.

> *"This sentence is by the decree of the angelic watchers And the decision is a command of the holy ones, So that the living may know [without any doubt] That the Most High [God] rules over the kingdom of mankind And He bestows it on whomever He desires And sets over it the humblest and lowliest of men." Dan. 4:17 Amp.*

Well, the problem is that there is not humility or lowliness ruling over our nations anymore.

This decree reflects the divine council's decision regarding this man. This is how it is expressed in the KJV.

> *This matter is by the decree of the watchers, (it has been decided) and the demand (a judicial decision) by the word (appointment) of the holy ones (angels) to the intent that the living may know that the most High ruleth in the kingdom of men, and giveth it to whomsoever he will, and setteth up over it the basest of men. Dan. 4:17 KJV (emphasis are mine)*

It is a decree from the watchers, which serves as a demand or judicial decision. This decree is an appointment bestowed by God's angelic beings.

A decree is an important order that carries the weight of the law, or it can be a religious directive established by a council or authority. It embodies a preordained intention or a *judicial decision*, often reflecting a decision made by divine guidance. This all sounds very much like the "Courtroom of Heaven!"

> *This is the dream which I, King Nebuchadnezzar, have seen. Now you, Belteshazzar, explain its meaning, since none of the wise men of my kingdom are able to reveal its interpretation to me; but you are able, for a spirit of the holy gods is in you.' Dan. 4:18*

Nebuchadnezzar recognizes that Daniel possesses a different spirit than all the other "wise men" who have come before the king and are unable to tell him the dream. He has faith that Daniel will have the answer. You and I walk in the same spirit that Daniel had. We must remember that if we are ever faced with a similar test, God will work through us as He did with Daniel. Although Daniel held a position of high esteem within the nation, we may not have risen to such a status. However, the role that each of us holds within our own circles will determine how the spirit of God reveals His secrets to us as they are needed.

This is a different circumstance from the situation with Ahab. He believed the lying prophets, but Nebuchadnezzar knew that the other wise men had no answers for him. He knows that there is one who has the spirit of God within him and is actually willing to listen.

> *"Then Daniel, whose [Babylonian] name was Belteshazzar, was appalled and speechless for a while [because he was deeply concerned about the destiny of the king], and his thoughts alarmed him. The king said, 'Belteshazzar, do not let the dream or its interpretation frighten you.' Belteshazzar answered, 'My lord, may the dream be [meant] for those who hate you and its message for your enemies! Dan. 4:19 Amp.*

Other translations say he was speechless for an hour. His thoughts alarmed him. That word alarmed is behal in the Hebrew. and it means his thoughts literally terrify Daniel.

Secret: Sometimes moving in the supernatural will leave you speechless!

Sometimes, when someone says something to you, you know exactly what it means, but it is so strong or powerful that it takes a while before you know how you are to speak it out. Daniel is appalled and speechless because he is deeply concerned about the destiny of the king.

> *The tree that you saw, which became great and grew strong, whose height reached to heaven and which was visible to all the earth, whose foliage was beautiful and its fruit abundant, and on which was food for all, under which the beasts of the field lived, and in whose branches the birds of the sky nested—Dan. 4:20-21*

Then he says, "It is you Oh King. The tree is you!"

> *it is you, O king, who have become great and grown strong; your greatness has increased and it reaches to heaven, and your dominion (kingdom) [reaches] to the ends of the earth. In that the king saw an angelic watcher, a holy one, descending from heaven and saying, "Cut the tree down and destroy it; but leave the stump with its roots in the earth, but with a band of iron and bronze around it in the new grass of the field, and let him be wet with the dew of heaven, and let this is a matter of the **divine council's decision** concerning this man. this is the interpretation, O king: It is the decree of the Most High [God], which has come upon my lord the king: Dan. 4:22-24*

Daniel is saying to the King, there is a decision from heaven that has been made about you. It is **already decreed**. An angel is executing a decree from God himself. It is a judgment that has come upon this king, leader of a great nation.

There is so much to learn from this story. When we think God doesn't see, we have no knowledge of what He already has in the works or what decrees have already been given.

> *that you shall be **driven** from mankind and your dwelling place shall be with the beasts of the field; and that you be given grass*

> *to eat like the cattle and be wet with the dew of heaven; and seven periods of time shall pass over you, until you know [without any doubt] that the Most High [God] rules over the kingdom of mankind and He bestows it to whomever He desires. Dan. 4:25*

This does not say men drive him away. It says he is driven from mankind. The angels are chasing him away from mankind. The word "driven," is terad in Hebrew, which means to expel; and to follow closely. That sounds like chasing to me.

To "know" is to certify, make known, and teach. It is Yedah in the Hebrew. There will be no question in the King's mind that God is the ruler over all the kingdoms of the earth.

God is dealing with the King's pride and arrogance. He is telling him, "You did not rise to greatness on your own."

> *And in that it was commanded to leave the stump with the roots of the tree [in the earth], your kingdom shall be restored to you after you recognize (understand fully) that Heaven rules. Dan. 4:26*

Heaven rules! Regardless of how large your kingdom becomes, how clever you think you are, or how much you believe you are a god, Heaven rules.

> *Therefore, O king, let my advice to you be [considered and found] acceptable; break away now from your sins and exhibit your repentance by doing what is right, and from your wickedness (perverseness) by showing mercy to the poor, so that [if you repent] there may possibly be a continuance of your prosperity and tranquility and a healing of your error.' Dan. 4:27*

Perverseness is defined as corruption, as being wicked or morally wrong. How much of that do we witness in our current world? Daniel is pleading with the King. "Please, King, repent now. Change your ways and humble yourself before this dream manifests in reality. Do something to show that you have turned away from your corruption. God is giving the King an opportunity for repentance, yet he doesn't take it."

Daniel tells him that the first thing he can do is show mercy to the poor. In America, we have so many homeless individuals that most of us can't even imagine what their lives are like. Justice calls for showing compassion to those in need and addressing people's basic needs. Stop misappropriating tax dollars from the less fortunate and redirecting them elsewhere to win votes. Quit making life harder for people.

He tells the King that if he repents, there may be a continuation of his prosperity and tranquility. God provides an opportunity to repent. God's people are crying out for justice, so the angels have been sent to assist them. We have no idea what has already been decreed from heaven for our nation.

> *"All this happened to Nebuchadnezzar the king. Dan. 4:28*

The King has been warned and has been given a whole year to turn things around.

> *Twelve months later he was walking on the upper level of the royal palace of Babylon. The king said thoughtfully, 'Is not this the great Babylon which I myself have built as the royal residence and seat of government by the might of my power and for the honor and glory of my majesty?' Dan. 4:29-30*

This reminds me of Herod in the New Testament. He stood on the balcony and allowed his constituents to call him a god. That's when the angels showed up again, and he was instantly eaten by worms.

Here we see Nebuchadnezzar doing the same thing. He proclaims, "Is not this greatness my own doing?" He claims it is for his honor, glory, magnificence, and majesty. He takes credit for everything.

Secret: *The sin of pride aligns you with the devil!*

The reason Babylon was able to conquer Israel was that Israel disobeyed God by refusing to let the land rest when He commanded them to. The land was supposed to rest every seven years, It was to have a Sabbath! This had not occurred for 490 years. As a result, Israel went into captivity for 70 years to allow the land the rest God had ordained. Another reason was that God instructed Israel to release their indentured servants after six years. During the time of Jeremiah, they agreed to release them but then went back and re-enslaved them, putting them back under bondage.

God never intended for Israel to be enslaved again. Once He freed them from bondage in Egypt, He desired for them to remain free forever. Instead, some of the Israelites began enslaving their own people. God used Babylon as a form of discipline and allowed them to conquer His people. Because they had enslaved their own people, God permitted them to be enslaved themselves.

God had withdrawn His protection from Israel and employed Babylon as a lesson for them. Therefore, it was not Nebuchadnezzar's greatness that led to his kingdom's prosperity but rather the sovereignty of God. Nebuchadnezzar was unwilling to share his glory with God or anyone else.

He is proclaiming his greatness. This is my majesty, my honor, my power. What we, as believers in Yeshua, strive for is to behold our King and become like Him. He is the greatest example of selfless love that exists! Pride is the reason for Satan's fall; it is also the reason for Nebuchadnezzar's. Pride always goes before a fall.

> *While the words were still in the king's mouth, a voice came [as if falling] from heaven, saying, 'O King Nebuchadnezzar, to you **it is declared**: "The kingdom has been removed from you, Dan. 4:31*

A command from heaven has come. He was given the chance to repent, and he did not. The opportunity for his repentance has passed, and he is being judged. This will be true for all of us. There will come a day when there is no more time. Time runs out for everyone! The decision will be made from heaven. Despite a man believing he is a god, it doesn't matter because he is not! No matter what he may think of himself.

> *and you will be **driven** away from mankind, and your dwelling place will be with the animals of the field. You will be given grass to eat like the cattle, and seven periods of time will pass over you until you know [without any doubt] that the Most High God rules over the kingdom of mankind and He bestows it on whomever He desires. Dan. 4:32*

When we look at who is driving him from mankind. It is the angels. This is how it reads in the CJB.

> *All who live on earth are counted as nothing. He does what he wishes with the **army of heaven** and with those living on earth. No one can hold back his hand or ask him, "What are you doing?" Dan. 4:32*

Army of Heaven. We are being assisted by the army of heaven. And no one in the universe can ask God, What are you doing?

> *Immediately the word concerning Nebuchadnezzar was fulfilled. He was **driven away** from mankind and began eating grass like cattle, and his body was wet with the dew of heaven until his hair had grown like eagles' feathers and his nails were like birds' claws. "But at the end of the days [that is, at the seven periods of time], I, Nebuchadnezzar, raised my eyes toward heaven, Dan. 4:33-34*

It looks like he is on all fours at this time and he is probably chained.

He says, "My understanding and reason returned to me; I blessed the Most High [God] and praised, honored, and glorified Him who lives forever. For His dominion is an everlasting dominion, and His kingdom endures from generation to generation."

There is only one God who deserves glory and honor. After seven years of being totally abased, the King comes to this knowing. He realizes who the real king is and by whom the eternal kingdom is ruled. This is King Nebuchadnezzar's confession.

> *"All the inhabitants of the earth are regarded as nothing. But He does according to His will in the **host of heaven** And among the inhabitants of the earth; And no one can hold back His hand Or say to Him, 'What have You done?' Dan. 4:35*

In the KJV, it reads:

> *And all the inhabitants of the earth are reputed as nothing: and he doeth according to his will in the **army of heaven**, and among the inhabitants of the earth: and none can stay his hand, or say unto him, What doest thou? Dan. 4:35*

God employs the heavenly host to interact with His earthly family.

The word "Army" is khah'-yil in Hebrew: it means strength, might, power, force, an army as a band of soldiers, company, forces, might, power, and war.

"Heaven" is shaw-mah'-yin in the Hebrew. celestial bodies

War was declared on Nebuchadnezzar from heaven, and he was chased from mankind.

> *Now at the same time my reason (intellect, understanding) returned to me; and for the glory of my kingdom, my majesty and splendor were returned to me, and my counselors and my nobles began seeking me out; so I was re-established in my kingdom, and still more greatness [than before] was added to me. Dan. 4:36*

It is like Job; his later end was better than in the beginning.

The word "established" is tek-an' in Hebrew, meaning to straighten up, to set in order. I wonder if this is also physical. Did he really straighten up after being on all fours, eating with the animals? That's why I believe he was crawling on his hands. He was clawing at the ground and eating the grass. How else could you do that if you weren't down on the ground on your hands and knees? But now he is established and set in order.

> *Now I, Nebuchadnezzar, praise and exalt and honor the King of heaven, for all His works are true and faithful and His ways are just, and He is able to humiliate and humble those who walk in [self-centered, self-righteous] pride." Dan. 4:37 Amp.*

He has certainly learned humility. God is giving prideful, arrogant, destructive, and self-centered people time to repent. We need to align ourselves with heaven for that to happen or for the time of judgment to come. There will be a day when no more time is left.

Once again, we have witnessed the Divine Counsel at work in the life of an earthly King. The angels have interacted with humanity. Heaven has mingled with earth. The cries of the people were heard, and the one causing their persecution was judged. The angels executed the decree and the judgment. They drove the King from the palace, and likely they were present to help free him when he was restored after his repentance. The courts of heaven are in order, and decrees are being continually issued on behalf of mankind. The angels are judging and executing judgment on behalf of Yahweh, Ruler of the Universe.

They watch our every move, they record our every word, they are ever present, and they are our fellow servants, bringing to earth the Kingdom of God!

In the Second Temple writings, we encounter terms such as "brigades of angels." The names of these angelic groups often have militaristic tones. A variety of combat-related terms are associated with angels, clearly portraying them as celestial warriors. They are seen warring alongside humans in the battle against evil. So, these historical books are reinforcing what we see in the scriptures with our fellow servants.

Secret: Pay attention: Someone unseen is in your midst.

So, what we know is that when God raises His hand to act against the wicked spirits, His angels prepare for battle. This is evident throughout the Word and the Apocrypha, including in the Dead Sea Scrolls. It's just amazing to me how much assistance we have that nobody has ever taught us about.

So, take heart. Nothing is getting past our King. He sees everything. We, however, need to be crying out.

> *And the glory of the God of Israel was gone up from the cherub, whereupon he was, to the threshold of the house. And he called to the man clothed with linen, which had the writer's inkhorn by his side; Ez. 9:3*

The man in white linen is an angel. He carries out the will of God just before destruction comes upon the city. He is marking those who belong to God. He is sealing us; we are his Bride!

> *And the LORD said unto him, Go through the midst of the city, through the midst of Jerusalem, and set a mark upon the foreheads of the men that sigh and that cry for all the abominations that be done in the midst thereof. Ez. 9:4*

Those are the ones God is marking. Those of us who cry out and pray for justice regarding the abominations we see occurring in our nation and in the nation of Israel. We witness the death of the innocent, the marketing and sex slavery, of human trafficking, and the imprisonment of the guiltless. We must cry out for justice. That's how the angel knows to mark us for God's Kingdom.

> *And to the others he said in mine hearing, Go ye after him through the city, and smite: let not your eye spare, neither have ye pity:*

Slay utterly old and young, both maids, and little children, and women: but come not near any man upon whom is the mark; and begin at my sanctuary. Then they began at the ancient men which were before the house. Ez 9:5-6

Secret: You have been sealed by God!

There is a mark that God is sealing us with. Those of us who are working with Him in warfare and praying for the innocent to be vindicated, for them to be set free, and for God to judge the guilty will receive God's mark. This occurs through our warfare and our prayers. The angels are constantly working with us. Side by side, when we go into battle, they fight alongside us.

We have a job to do. We cannot look at what is happening and accept it, saying that we can't stop what is already written. We are still required to cry out about it. We are called to a battle!

Chapter 13

Joshua

Look around. What do you see? Now, quiet yourself and close your eyes. What do you sense/feel? We often perceive something around us, even if we can't see it.

Is the idea of the supernatural frightening for you? Do you experience fear when it comes to embracing the unseen realm? It's okay if you don't see or sense the presence of God's unseen family. They are faithful to support you if you are an heir of salvation.

Since childhood, we've heard that angels exist. However, this reality has not impacted most of us in any practical or personal way. We don't fully understand what is available to us. We fail to recognize that we have guardians, friends, and companions by our side every day, and they have been with us since birth.

This is not just an imaginary friend from childhood! These are partners assigned to you to help navigate this maze called life.

The first time I learned about angels was when I was about four years old and heard the story of Jesus's birth, where the angels appeared. However, no one ever told me that they would show up for me, in any way.

It's perfectly fine to talk to them and thank them for everything they do. While I believe it's not our place to command them, I understand that we can request their assistance much more often than we do. The Word of God states that they are fellow servants. They want to see the Kingdom of God come to earth, just like we do. We are on assignment together.

We have received so much through the blood of Yeshua/Jesus. He has provided us with everything that pertains to life and godliness.

> *According as his divine power hath given unto us all things that pertain unto life and godliness, through the knowledge of him that hath called us to glory and virtue: 2 Peter 1:3*

When I began to write this chapter, I asked the Lord what he wanted to say to you, the reader. He said, "I want to tell them how very much I love them. That I am rooting for them to be faithful until the end."

Secret: It is the one who finishes the race that receives the prize!

He is starting to remove certain individuals from our lives. He is distancing those who may hinder you as you navigate the trials associated with the end of days. He is not severing relationships, but he is creating space from you as a form of protection.

Secret: Some people are no longer part of your life for your own protection!

Often, we yearn for close relationships with those we love. However, many of these individuals have not committed themselves to wholeheartedly following the Lord. They will not walk this journey with you. The Father desires for those who hold our hands to encourage us in our spiritual walk. We are meant to surround ourselves with like-minded people and share this journey together until the very end.

People have speculated that America was supposed to have more time before the darkness became so prevalent. They believe that Satan has speeded up his agenda because he knows his time is short. He has a mission to complete and only has so much time allotted to him on this earth.

> *……..the devil is come down unto you, having great wrath, because he knoweth that he hath but a short time. Rev. 12:12*

As we continue our walk through the Word, exploring many of the manifestations of angelic assistance in our warfare, we can be assured that no matter where we are in time, we are being watched. God has assigned angels to each one of His children. Hopefully, understanding this will make our sojourning easier as we travel these pilgrim highways on this earth.

Remember that God never calls us His adults. We are and always will be His children. We were assigned angels at birth, and nothing has changed. In this earthly realm, we consider ourselves grown-ups, but God still sees us as His children with the same angels we had from the day we were born.

> *Take heed that ye despise not one of these little ones; for I say unto you, That in heaven their **angels** do always behold the face of my Father which is in heaven. Matt. 18:10*

We're about to take a journey through the amazing victory at Jerico, as Joshua takes on the leadership role for Israel, after the death of Moses. Joshua faced the challenge of leading all of Israel—around two million people—across the Jordan River, which was no small feat.

Now after the death of Moses the servant of the LORD it came to pass, that the LORD spake unto Joshua the son of Nun, Moses' minister, saying, Jos. 1:1

This is God, YHVH himself, the self-existing one, speaking to Joshua just as He spoke to Moses. It doesn't tell us if He spoke out of the cloud, but that seems logical since that is how we've seen Him communicating with Israel up to this point—through the cloud over the tabernacle they built for worship. If you remember, each time Moses entered the Tabernacle, Joshua accompanied him and stayed at the entrance of the tent. He never left Moses's side. God kept speaking to Joshua, saying:

> *Moses my servant is dead; now therefore arise, go over this Jordan, thou, and all this people, unto the land which I do give to them, even to the children of Israel. Jos. 1:2*

This next word, "Now," really caught my attention. The word "Now" means straightway; at this time, there is no more delay.

He took everyone with him except the wives and children of Reuben, Gad, and half the tribe of Manasseh. God is giving them the land that was promised hundreds of years before to His faithful servant, Abraham. It is finally happening! They have been sojourning for four hundred thirty years, holding onto their faith in God for this very moment for a long time, and it's finally going to happen.

This almost brings me to tears. This has been promised to Abraham and his descendants for so long, and it will finally be fulfilled. So, when it states that the meek shall inherit the earth or that God is giving us the land, it is monumental! These people have been humbled, enslaved, and wandered in the wilderness for forty years. Now, God will part the Jordan for Joshua, just as He parted the Red Sea for Moses. Our God is truly a God of miracles!

Secret: Humbling often leads to victory!

Abraham was willing to sacrifice everything precious to him to have this covenant relationship with Yahweh. He believed in the promise. The book of Hebrews tells us that the patriarchs died without seeing the promise, but God never forgot His part of the covenant.

> *These all died in faith, not having received the promises, but having seen them afar off, and were persuaded of them, and embraced them, and **confessed** that they were strangers and pilgrims on the earth. Heb. 11:13*

Abraham continued to confess what God had promised. He never doubted God, and God is honoring His Word. He promised Abraham that He would make his descendants like the stars in the heavens and the sands of the sea and that He would give him the land. Abraham sojourned in Canaan for years, and the whole time, God was saying, "This is your land!

Walk the length and breadth of it, and everywhere you place your foot, I will give it to you."

God is not only speaking this to Joshua; He is speaking it to us today. For those of us who endure to the end, we will inherit the earth. We begin by living in the millennial reign in Jerusalem with Yeshua. We inherit the land through the blood and the promise of Yeshua/Jesus. Later, there will be a completely new heaven and earth that comes down from heaven. That promise is for us. We also have a promise of inheritance.

Jesus said:

> *I assure you and most solemnly say to you, many prophets and righteous men [who were honorable and in right standing with God] longed to see what you see, and did not see it, and to hear what you hear, and did not hear it. Matt. 13:17 Amp.*

They longed to witness what we now look back on: the Messiah walking the earth, shining as a light to the Gentiles, uniting all of Israel under one king, the Messiah/Yeshua/Jesus.

The many prophets included Daniel, Ezekiel, Isaiah, Jeremiah, and Zechariah. They could see the new heaven and the new earth, and although they never fully understood it, they longed to see its fulfillment. They desired to see the Messiah.

> *The prophets, who prophesied about this gift of deliverance (grace, Yeshua) that was meant for you, pondered and inquired diligently about it. 1 Pe. 1:10*

We have the privilege of looking back and now understanding what the prophets were seeing then. I find myself saying to the Lord, "Teach me, God. Teach me what all these future prophecies mean. How is the future going to unfold, and when will it occur? Please teach me; please speak to me. Speak to my heart so I will understand. That is the same kind of thing that the prophets of old were saying then."

The prophet, Daniel, witnessed things that made him feel physically ill, and the angel instructed him to shut the book and seal it until the end of time, indicating that it wasn't the right moment for him to understand. What he saw was a long way off for Daniel, but it isn't far off for you and me. Now is the time. Peter explains what this was like for the prophets.

> *Searching what, or what manner of time the Spirit of Christ which was in them did signify, when it testified beforehand the sufferings of Christ, and the glory that should follow. 1 Pet. 1:11*

They prophesied Jesus' suffering but never understood when, why, or how. It states that the spirit of the Messiah was already within them. Their question was how the Messiah would endure suffering yet still experience all the glorious things that were to follow. How were they supposed to understand that?

They were looking forward to the Savior coming, yet it was difficult to comprehend. Looking back makes understanding much easier for us. We can see that he was a suffering servant and yet is a ruling King. We have the benefits of the new birth and the infilling of the Holy Spirit. We have the New Testament, which provides great explanations of what the Torah and the Prophets were trying to convey. They sought diligently to understand this. They prophesied his suffering, but they didn't grasp it. When? Why? How?

> *It was revealed to them that their services [their prophecies regarding grace] were not [meant] for themselves and their time, but for you, in these things [the death, resurrection, and glorification of Jesus Christ] which have now been told to you by those who preached the gospel to you by the [power of the] Holy Spirit [who was] sent from heaven. Into these things even the angels long to look. 1 Pe. 1:12*

Even the angels are excited. They sense something is about to happen, but they don't know why or when. They know Yeshua/Jesus will reclaim this Earth.

> *And the seventh angel sounded; and there were great voices in heaven, saying, The kingdoms of this world are become the kingdoms of our Lord, and of his Christ; and he shall reign for ever and ever. Rev. 11:15*
>
> *The earth is the Lords and the fullness thereof. Ps. 24:1*

It is the systems of the Earth that have been destroyed by the demonic forces of Satan himself. However, God will reclaim it all, and even the angels long to look into these matters. They possess a desire and passion to understand just as we do.

Secret: Satan does not own the earth! Only it's kingdoms.

Jesus will reclaim this earth! Just as we anticipate Yeshua's return today, they looked for the promise of the land given to Abraham. Now it is about to happen as Joshua leads Israel, across the Jordan River, guided by Our Conquering King and His angels!

> *Every place that the sole of your foot shall tread upon, that have I given unto you, as I said unto Moses. Jos. 1:3*

God told Abraham this as well; right after the destruction of Sodom and Gomorrah, He said to Abraham, "I want you to walk through this land. I want you to examine it closely, for every place you walk, I am going to give it to you." That was the promise to Abraham, and then it was passed to Moses; now it is given to Joshua and all the children of Israel.

> *No man will [be able to] stand before you [to oppose you] as long as you live. Just as I was [present] with Moses, so will I be with you; I will not fail you or abandon you. (His presence is going with him.) Be strong and confident and courageous, for you will*

> *give this people as an inheritance the land which I swore to their fathers (ancestors) to give them. Jos 1:5-6 Amp*

He swore it to them. The word be strong is *khaw-zak'* in the Hebrew (Strongs H2388), which means to be fortified, to be obstinate, to conquer, to be constant, to be established, to prevail, to behave self valiantly.

Obstinate like you are refusing to give up. He is determined to take the land and to take it now. There will be no more turning back. We will do what God told us to do or die. We will see God's promises fulfilled. Look at all that Khawzak means. That's what God is calling us to do as well. To behave like a warrior, valiantly.

> *Only be strong and very courageous; be careful to do [everything] in accordance with the entire law which Moses My servant commanded you; do not turn from it to the right or to the left, so that you may prosper and be successful wherever you go. Jos. 1:7*

Very courageous is *aw-mats'* in the Hebrew (Strongs H553) which means *steadfastly minded, establish, fortify, to be harden, to prevail, to strengthen self.*

Secret: Obedience makes your way prosperous!

What makes his way prosperous is doing everything in God's way. Continually following Moses's ways will ensure good success. He is told not to turn to the right or to the left and to be sure to observe everything according to the law of Moses. He doesn't get to pick and choose. It's not about what he believes is right or wrong; it's about what God says is right or wrong. His Word has the final say.

Often, we hear people say, "Well, that's not what it means to me!" when referring to a particular scripture. If you look at how Jesus walked and do the same, you won't go astray. Just as Joshua was told to follow Moses' ways, we are told to follow Jesus. He is forever the same!

In the next verse, God repeats himself. When we see something written twice, it is for emphasis. It is being said in the strongest of manners

> *This Book of the Law shall not depart from your mouth, but you shall read [and meditate on] it day and night, so that you may be careful to do [everything] in accordance with all that is written in it; for then you will make your way prosperous, and then you will be successful. Jos. 1:8*

God's Word is not to depart out of Joshua's mouth. We are to speak it. Words have power. So, what is he supposed to do? Read and meditate and speak. If the Word is in your heart, it will come out of your mouth automatically. Out of the abundance of the heart, the mouth speaketh.

> *......for out of the abundance of the heart the mouth speaketh. Mat.12:34*

God is emphatic about our meditation and adherence to the Word. He emphasizes in two consecutive verses that it guarantees success. When we focus on everything God has said, we prosper and have success.

To meditate on the Word is to chew it, to ponder it, to think deeply about it.

> *Have I not commanded you? Be strong and courageous! Do not be terrified or dismayed (intimidated), for the LORD your God is with you wherever you go." Jos. 1:9*

That is why I am writing this book: the angels of Yahweh are with us wherever we go. They are your constant companions, whether you know it or not.

Secret: *We are commanded to be courageous!*

God warns Joshua not to repeat the mistakes the Hebrews made 40 years earlier. They were intimidated, dismayed, and terrified. God instructed Joshua, saying, "Don't be like that!" When the twelve spies first entered the land, they brought back enormous clusters of grapes and huge pomegranates, proclaiming it was a land flowing with milk and honey! Yet, they were still fearful. They saw giants in the land and proclaimed, "We look like grasshoppers to ourselves." They felt as if they could be easily crushed under the feet of these giants. We cannot view ourselves as grasshoppers. We are not insects waiting for the enemy to crush us.

We are who God says we are! We are brave, daring, and unafraid! We will take the land, just as He commanded Joshua to do.

So, this is what Joshua did: he sent out spies who ended up on the roof of Rahab's house. Most of us know this story. This time, he sends out only two spies instead of twelve, which makes more sense. It's easier to reach an agreement between two than among twelve. He didn't need twelve voices and everyone with an opinion. Here is what Rahab said to them.

> *"I know that the LORD has given you the land, and that the terror and dread of you has fallen on us, and that all the inhabitants of the land have melted [in despair] because of you. Jos. 2:9*

What she doesn't understand is that the terror is not because of the Israelites; it is because of their Great God!

Do you remember God sending a lying spirit into the mouths of 400 prophets to Ahab? Well, this time, He has sent a spirit of terror and dread upon Canaan. Remember, there are giants in this land. This time, it's the giants that are fearful and filled with terror. How did this happen?

Consider this: Angels are spirits. They can sometimes appear as humans, and at other times, they can manifest as spirits to influence humanity for God's purposes. In the chapter "The Divine Counsel," a lying spirit spoke from the mouths of all the prophets to Ahab. That was an angel sent as a lying spirit. Likewise, the spirit of dread and terror has now fallen upon all of Canaan. It is an angelic spirit sent in the form of fear and dread to paralyze the enemy.

This is something we must keep in mind as we see fear fall on whole communities in the days ahead. Realize what you are dealing with and speak peace to it.

Rahab tells the spies that Canaan has heard of all that Yahweh has done; she is already a believer at this point. Most people have never caught this. But this is what it says in verse 11:

> *When we heard, our hearts melted in despair. A fighting spirit no longer remained in any man because their will to fight was gone.* ***For the Lord your God, He is God*** *in heaven above and on the earth beneath. Jos. 2:11*

She has already decided who her God is. She acknowledges and recognizes that the God of Israel is God Almighty and that there is no other besides Him! When we look at the word "harlot," it doesn't necessarily mean that she is a prostitute; it indicates that she had been an adulteress, which was probably common in her society. She was living in an extremely corrupt environment. We don't know how the spies ended up at her house, but we know she is already a believer. It seems that God Himself has directed the spies to a place of safety. All of this helps us better understand why she would be willing to hide the spies and put her own life in jeopardy.

Rahab let the spies down over the wall, putting her own life in great danger; the men of Canaan were already searching for them, and she knew it. Before the Hebrew spies escaped over the wall, they agreed to spare her and her family when they invaded the land.

The spies returned to report to Joshua:

> *They said to Joshua, "Certainly the LORD has given all the land into our hands; for all the inhabitants of the land have melted [in despair] because of us. Jos. 2:24*

Do you see the contrast between the report of these two spies compared to the fearful report of the twelve, forty years before? God has done a miraculous work in these people as they endured the hardships of the desert. This is a nation of mighty warriors fit for battle. They are indeed the Lord's Army here on earth!

Joshua began preparing to take an entire nation across the Jordan River. Remember, God opened up the Red Sea for Moses; now we see that God will open the Jordan River for Joshua. This is done in a completely different way than it was for Moses. It is no less miraculous! These were Joshua's instructions to Israel:

> *And they commanded the people, saying, When ye see the ark of the covenant of the LORD your God, and the priests the Levites bearing it, then ye shall remove from your place, and go after it. Yet there shall be a space between you and it, about two thousand cubits by measure: come not near unto it, that ye may know the way by which ye must go: for ye have not passed this way heretofore. Jos. 3:3-4*

I wondered if the ark was covered. Only the High Priest was ever permitted to see it, and that was only once a year, behind a cloud of incense smoke. So, I'm guessing that as it entered the Jordan, it was still under its covering.

Remember when David brought the Ark of the Covenant into Jerusalem? It was being carried on a cart that began to wobble. Uzzah reached out his hand to steady the cart, and he instantly died when he touched it. God had given specific instructions on how the Ark was to be moved. We don't get to do things our own way when it comes to the Holiness of God!

When crossing the Jordan, Joshua instructed the people to follow the Ark while keeping a distance of 3,000 feet from it. Even though they were to keep their distance, they were not to lose sight of it because they hadn't passed this way before.

Well, guess what? We have not passed this way before, either. We don't understand all that we see; we don't know what's coming next. We can't tell if what we see is real anymore! Keep your eyes on the presence of Yeshua/Jesus. No one knows the true way for sure. We are in strange territory. Our days and times have never been walked through before. But just as He guided Israel through the Jordan and into the battle, He will guide us if we do not look to the right or to the left. We are not to be in fear or intimidated.

We are living in days when we don't know what is in the sky. We don't understand what is in the sea. Are they aliens? Are they orbs? Are they fallen angels? What's in the fog? What's being sprayed from the sky? What is in the injection? We have never walked this way before!

Joshua instructed the priest, "When you get to the edge of the Jordan, stand still." This is what happened as soon as their feet were submerged in the water:

> *the waters which were flowing down from above stopped and rose up in one mass a great distance away at Adam, the city that is beside Zarethan. Those [waters] flowing downward toward the sea of the Arabah, the Salt Sea, were completely cut off. So the people crossed [the river] opposite Jericho. And while all [the people of] Israel crossed over on dry ground, the priests who carried the ark of the covenant of the LORD stood firm on dry ground in the midst of the Jordan [riverbed], until all the nation had finished crossing over the Jordan. Jos. 3:16-17 Amp.*

Then Joshua commanded twelve men to bring twelve stones from the midst of the Jordan to set up a pillar to mark the crossing. This crossing was completely different from the Red Sea crossing, where God caused the winds to blow all night to separate the waters. This time, it was instant, requiring the spiritual leaders to step into the water with the Ark.

I wonder how many people were wondering what in the world is Joshua up to now. Does that crazy guy really believe that we are all going across the Jordan on dry ground? Who does he think he is? Moses? Or perhaps they had learned to keep quiet and wait to witness the glory of the Lord!

How incredible is this! Can you see it? Imagine being there. Talk about God showing off! This stuff is so astonishing that I wonder if the Hebrews went to sleep that night asking each other, "What did we just witness? Did that really happen?"

Everyone understood that it was the holy presence of the Ark of the Covenant that caused the waters to part and dry land to appear. Jesus said, "The things that I do, you will do greater." We see a type of this with Joshua and Moses. When Moses dried up the Red Sea, it took all night to bring forth the dry land. But with Joshua, it was immediate. Oh, what an amazing God we serve.

> *When the priests who carried the ark of the covenant of the LORD had come up from the midst of the Jordan, and the soles of their feet were raised up to the dry land, the waters of the Jordan returned to their place, and flowed over all its banks as before. Jos. 4:18*

This occurs during the river's flood season; it overflowed its banks. It's not just a small stream. The priest stood in the middle of the Jordan until every person had crossed over.

Consider this: we are called to be a kingdom of priests to our God. This is what Yahweh expected of His priests: courage, valor, and the stamina to remain steadfast until every person has crossed over. They did not move until Joshua commanded them. If Christ lives in you, are you now the Ark of the New Testament? Will His very presence within you open paths to lead others to the promised land of eternity with Jesus?

Secret: *You are the Ark of the New Testament!*

God tells us why He did this for Israel:

> *so that all the peoples of the earth may know [without any doubt] and acknowledge that the hand of the LORD is mighty and extraordinarily powerful, so that you will fear the LORD your God [and obey and worship Him with profound awe and reverence] forever. Jos. 4:24 Amp*

He desires all humanity to recognize His greatness, fear Him, and follow His commands. We are meant to be captivated by Him, to fall in love with Him, and to hold deep reverence for Him.

> *And it came to pass, when all the kings of the Amorites, which were on the side of Jordan westward, and all the kings of the Canaanites, which were by the sea, heard that the LORD had dried up the waters of Jordan from before the children of Israel, until we were passed over, that their heart melted, neither was there spirit in them anymore, because of the children of Israel. Jos. 5:1*

Because Israel has a God like no other! He sent a spirit of dread, terror, and fear before Israel entered Canaan. Then, He demonstrated His great power in the miraculous dividing of the Jordan. It's understandable that the Philistines later wanted to capture the Ark; they thought it had some kind of magic. But it wasn't magic! It was the presence of the God of the Universe. It contained God's instructions, which are the very essence of God's character, written on stone tablets.

His hand is not waxed short to meet every need in your life. To him is power and glory forever and ever.

> *Behold, the LORD's hand is not shortened, That it cannot save; Nor His ear heavy, That it cannot hear. Is. 59:1*

Before going into battle, God instructed Joshua to circumcise every male and to remain camped until they were all healed. Circumcision was the sign given to Abraham by God. They were about to receive all that was promised in that covenant, so they were required to bear the mark in their flesh, signifying to whom they belonged. This was God's family, distinct and set apart from all other people on Earth.

> *This day have I rolled away the reproach of Egypt. (Disgrace and shame).... Jos. 5:9*

This is what God says on the day they are all circumcised. Before entering the promised land, every male will bear the mark of the covenant in his own body. It serves as a constant reminder that they are in covenant with the God of Israel.

They stayed in Gilgal to celebrate Passover. This marks the last time they had manna, which was never seen again. This must have been an incredible celebration, and their expectations were undoubtedly high. They had witnessed God among them and were remembering the spectacular deliverance from Egypt. It had been forty years since their liberation.

God had provided for them throughout the wilderness, and now they were about to eat from the land that God promised to Abraham. After four hundred years of waiting, they would finally inhabit houses they didn't build and enjoy vineyards they didn't plant. They would reap the benefits of crops they didn't sow and were set to enjoy the finest of everything because God was granting it to them.

Israel was geared up and ready to fight. They are thrilled that the inhabitants of the land are in terror because of them. They have witnessed the miracle of the splitting of the Jordan, and they are prepared to take the land, fully aware that they are not going in alone. It is evident that their expectations are very high.

> *And it came to pass, when Joshua was by Jericho, that he lifted up his eyes and looked, and, behold, there stood a man over against him with his sword drawn in his hand: and Joshua went*

> *unto him, and said unto him, Art thou for us, or for our adversaries? (Opposite him) Jos. 5:13*

This angel has his sword drawn! The Word doesn't reveal many details about him. However, there are some obvious questions that we might consider. How large is this angel in human form? Joshua asked him if he was for the adversary. Jerico is full of giants! I have seen some enormous angels, so my first thought is that this might be why Joshua wanted to know which side he was on. Did he appear to be a giant? I suspect that this angelic being is quite large. Joshua wants to be sure whose side he is on.

> *And he said, Nay; but as **captain of the host of the LORD** am I now come. And Joshua fell on his face to the earth, and did worship, and said unto him, What saith my lord unto his servant? Jos. 5:14*

"Now! Now I have arrived. Now I am ready to assist." The time you have waited for is here! This is angelic aid in warfare. What I find intriguing about this angel is that he never tells Joshua, "Don't worship me. Get up off your face." We never see him say that, even though in other parts of Scripture, people are instructed not to bow before angels. What makes this angel different? Is he the same angel who visited Manoah? This angel is THE Captain of the host of the Lord!

In the book of Revelation, we learn that angels are our fellow servants and that we should not worship them. So, who is this angel? Is this the pre-incarnate Christ himself?

This is a high-ranking angel. In Hebrew, Captain is "sar" (head person of any rank or class: chief, general, governor, master, prince, ruler) of the armies of God.

The word "Host" is tsâbâ' tsebâ'âh in Hebrew it means a mass of persons organized for war, an army, soldiers waiting upon warfare.

This is Angelic Assistance coming to aid the Army of Israel in battle. Joshua is now aware of exactly who is going before him. God promised He would lead them to victory, and He has appeared to do just that.

He declares, "I am leading the army of the self-existing one, Yahweh!"

> *And the captain of the LORD'S host said unto Joshua, Loose thy shoe from off thy foot; for the place whereon thou standest is holy. And Joshua did so. Jos. 5:15*

Does this remind you of Moses at the burning bush? Joshua removes his shoes, unaware that he is on holy ground.

Secret: We don't always recognize that our surroundings are Holy!

One thing we know about the priesthood is that they never wore shoes in the presence of God. When we're told in Ephesians that our feet are shod with the preparation of the gospel of peace, it never mentions anything about shoes. The priest went barefoot in the Temple. We are called to be priests; perhaps our armor does not include shoes. Why would it if we are priests unto our God?

Joshua didn't realize he was on holy ground, nor did Moses. God, help us to be aware when we are in Your presence and in the presence of Your holy ones. Help us to remain alert and discerning of Your spirit.

One of the places where an angel of God stood unnoticed was with Balaam and the donkey. An angel was blocking his path, ready to kill him. I would never want to face an angel's anger for defying the voice of God.

The inhabitants of Jericho were so fearful that they had barricaded themselves inside. Remember, there are still giants in this land.

> *Yericho had completely barricaded its gates against the people of Isra'el—no one left, and no one entered. Jos. 6:1 CJB*

They are locked up tighter than a drum. When the Lord sends a spirit of terror on a city, no one takes any chances.

Secret: God will instill fear in your enemy!

> *And the LORD said unto Joshua, See, I have given into thine hand Jericho, and the king thereof, and the mighty men of valour. And ye shall compass the city, all ye men of war, and go round about the city once. Thus shalt thou do six days. Jos. 6:2-3*

This reminds me of creation; for six days, God works, and on the seventh is victory, a day of completion. It brings to mind the six millennial years, and on the seventh is victory. This marching follows the patterns of God.

> *And seven priests shall bear before the ark seven trumpets of rams' horns: and the seventh day ye shall compass the city seven times, and the priests shall blow with the trumpets. Jos. 6:4*

Once more, the ark is brought into the battle— a spiritual battle while crossing the Jordan and a physical battle against the enemy.

> *And it shall come to pass, that when they make a long blast with the ram's horn, and when ye hear the sound of the trumpet, all the people shall shout with a great shout; and the wall of the city shall fall down flat, and the people shall ascend up every man straight before him. And Joshua the son of Nun called the priests, and said unto them, Take up the ark of the covenant, and let seven priests bear seven trumpets of rams' horns before the ark of the LORD. Jos. 6:5-6*

Joshua is told to encircle the city completely. And on the seventh day the walls will fall down flat. Does that sound crazy or what? God's ways often don't make sense to mankind.

> *And he said unto the people, Pass on, and compass the city, and let him that is armed pass on before the ark of the LORD. And it came to pass, when Joshua had spoken unto the people, that the*

> *seven priests bearing the seven trumpets of rams' horns passed on before the LORD, and blew with the trumpets: and the ark of the covenant of the LORD followed them. And the armed men went before the priests that blew with the trumpets, and the rereward came after the ark, the priests going on, and blowing with the trumpets. And Joshua had commanded the people, saying, Ye shall not shout, nor make any noise with your voice, neither shall any word proceed out of your mouth, until the day I bid you shout; then shall ye shout Jos. 6:7-10*

No noise, no talking. They march in total silence, anticipating the moment when they will be told to shout! Don't you think they are wondering what it will be like when we shout? The silence must have unnerved the enemy.

> *And it came to pass on the seventh day, that they rose early about the dawning of the day, and compassed the city after the same manner seven times: only on that day they compassed the city seven times. And it came to pass at the seventh time, when the priests blew with the trumpets, Joshua said unto the people, Shout; for the LORD hath given you the city. Jos. 6:15-16*

God has given us the Kingdom; we should want to shout! We are a Kingdom of priests unto our God. He has bestowed His Kingdom upon us! He lives in us, and that Kingdom abides within us even now.

> *So the people shouted when the priests blew with the trumpets: and it came to pass, when the people heard the sound of the trumpet, and the people shouted with a great shout, that the wall fell down flat, so that the people went up into the city, every man straight before him, and they took the city. Jos. 6:20*

I can imagine this Angelic General leading them as they enter the land, just as God promised from the beginning. The Apocrypha tells us how angels and mankind fight together. They are with us side by side. They are our family, supporting us in every battle!

Did you ever wonder how those walls fell down flat? Was it the noise frequency from all the blowing and shouting? I doubt it. Or was it the man (angel) with his sword drawn, standing on holy ground, with his massive angelic army prepared for war? He is the Captain of the **Host**!

The Hebrews were required to fight. God didn't just do this for them. They had to enter the battle. They most certainly had unseen assistance. If we are watching, we see this in our own lives. This seems to be one of the things that the angels do on a regular basis.

More than once, we have witnessed two cars on the highway that should have collided. They occupied the same space at the same time without crashing. How does that happen? It's only possible because of the angels. They operate miraculously and are with us all the time. My husband and I recently experienced this twice while we were in one lane on the highway, and the vehicle next to us unexpectedly moved into our lane. For a split second, both cars occupied the same space. It was physically impossible for us not to crash, yet both cars remained unharmed. This must be an angelic intervention! When we see things like this, it boggles our minds! But why should it? We are meant to live a supernatural life!

Secret: Angels accompany the blast of the shofar!*

The blowing of the shofar is a "Heavenly call." I have always been told that it summons the angels. Spiritually, shofars are weapons, and their sounds alert the soul to an awakening.

Whenever you hear the shofar sound, it signifies the presence of God. This was the exact sound that came from the thick cloud on Mount Sinai in the Exodus. The blowing of the shofar marks the arrival of God. Remember when the shofar sounded and shook the whole mountain in the book of Exodus?

*Fromtheangels.com *Chadbad.org says that Satan stands at the right side to accuse a person before G-d. Among other things, the piercing blasts of the shofar serve to "confuse" Satan. (I like that!)

The shofar will announce the return of Yeshua for His Saints, accompanied by a host of angels. In American cowboy and Indian movies, we often witness the blowing of the trumpet to summon the cavalry. When we sound the shofar, we call forth the angelic cavalry.

I'm confident that the blowing and shouting at Jerico must have confused the enemy. It was completely silent for seven days, and then, all at once, there was a blast that surely shook the walls, everything, and everyone inside the city.

Individuals who practice karate are instructed to release a shout when they strike. Loud sounds can catch people by surprise.

> *And He will send out His angels with a loud **trumpet** call, and they will gather His elect from the four winds, from one end of the heavens to the other. Matt. 24:31*

So, we see that angels accompany the blast of the shofar.

> *For this we say unto you by the word of the Lord, that we which are alive and remain unto the coming of the Lord shall not prevent them which are asleep. For the Lord himself shall descend from heaven with a **shout**, with the voice of the **archangel**, and with the **trump** of God: and the dead in Christ shall rise first: 1 Th. 4:15-16*

Again, we see angels accompanying the blast of the shofar, which is so loud that it will wake up and raise the dead!

> *Then we which are alive and remain shall be caught up together with them in the clouds, to meet the Lord in the air: and so shall we ever be with the Lord. 1 Th. 4:17*

No more separation. No more veil between us; we are ever with the Lord!

I wept while writing this chapter. The thought that we may be the generation to witness the sky splitting and the Mount of Olives separating when Jesus/Yeshua places His foot upon it is simply overwhelming. We are they! Israel witnessed the splitting of the Red Sea, the rock that poured out water, and the Jordan River parting so they could cross on dry land.

But we will see our own splitting! I believe we are that generation! The time is drawing near. We have come to this day. It is Jesus who is opening the seals. We need to rejoice about that. Our redemption is drawing near. Even so, Lord Jesus/Yeshua come!

Hopefully you have begun to realize that living a supernatural life is normal for every Christian. We will see you in Volume Two.

Bibliography

e-Sword -The Sword of the Lord with an electronic edge with commentaries, dictionaries, and teachings of the early fathers.

Michael Heiser, "Angels."

https://www.merriam-webster.com/dictionary/restraint

Ant. 5:1:17, and http://nazarenespace.com/blog/2020/12/21/the-lost-book-of-jasher-and-the-dead-sea-scrolls/

https://www.chabad.org/multimedia/timeline_cdo/aid/525324/jewish/June-8-Day-4.htm

https://cbnisrael.org/2022/06/09/fulfilling-gods-promises-the-miracles-of-israels-six-day-war/

Michael S. Heiser, Unseen Realm, Lexham Press, 2015, pg.133.

www.delightfulknowledge.com/hidden-name-of-creator-in-your-dna

Descriptions of Angels: (1) Is.14:29, (2) Ez.1:10, 10:14, 41:18-19 (3) Eph. 1:21,3:10, 6:12, Rm. 8:38, Col. 1:16,

Fromtheangels.com *Chadbad.org: Satan stands at the right side to accuse a person before G-d. Among other things, the piercing blasts of the shofar serve to "confuse" Satan.

Secrets by Chapter:

Introduction:

The wounds of your past blur your Spiritual Vision

God has Two Families.

We can be in two places at once.

Chapter 1

You don't have to understand what you see in the Spirit to exercise authority over it!

The Devil goes to Church.

Demons are assigned to congregations.

Chapter 2

The Devil's Greatest Weapon Is His Mouth

Our spiritual armor doesn't resemble that of a Roman soldier

Practice makes perfect!

There is a hidden force behind your daily struggles!

Satan's food is the force of iniquity!

Things go better when you read the instructions!

Gathering with others to pray or do warfare multiplies your power exponentially!

You will be held accountable for every word spoken!

If the devil can't get to you, he will find someone else who can.

You can reverse the curse!

Chapter 3

Three Angels can appear as 2000 men.

Things that happen in the spirit may manifest in the physical.

God doesn't need to reveal how He works on YOUR behalf. He simply does it!

Angels will speak for you!

You are never too old to have guardian angels (more than one).

Chapter 4

The Word of God is filled with hidden Gems. It is the glory of God to conceal a thing, but the honor of kings to search out a matter. Pr. 25:2

Worship is part of Warfare!

Mercy comes with repentance!

Angels are sent to bring you wisdom in the war.

Sometimes, you get more than you bargained for when the angels appear

Revelations that are not understood may arise from your spiritual warfare!

Some of God's angels are frightening

The presence of angels can make you weak!

Angels come for your Words!

Your words, prayers, and warfare hold tremendous power!

Chapter 5

Our Words are Weapons

This Battle is A War of Words. Words are Containers That Hold Power.

Not only are good angels moved by your words, but so are the evil ones!

God's name is on your DNA!

Remembering the day you were saved strengthens your resolve for the upcoming battle.

If You Ask God More Questions, You Get More Answers

Satan thrives on iniquity; don't nourish him with your WORDS of agreement!

Chapter 6

Angels Rescue in Personal Conflicts

Sometimes Angels Come Looking for You.

Your personal victory could change the fate of a nation.

When the devil attacks you by using another person, YOU may request Angel Armies to assist you in your personal battles.

God Doesn't just Win Battles. He Takes Back What the Devil Stole.

Chapter 7

Get it in your spirit that God sees and knows everything. Nothing escapes Him!

Pay attention: The supernatural of Satan is a copy of Our God. Nothing is original to him.

Did you know blinding the enemy is one of the angel's weapons?

A strategic weapon in warfare may require a lie!

You can ask for angels to chase the enemy and to persecute them.

Angels bring healing.

Chapter 8

Worship is a form of warfare!

The enemy shows no fear in insulting God. Respond as Hezekiah did!

The violent take it by force!

If you participate in the things of this world, it will vex your soul!

Chapter 9

Soaking in the presence of God sharpens your spiritual senses.

Being a Christian is supernatural! Do you realize that?

Understanding the Holiness of God will cause you to tremble.

At times, being separated from family or social circles can be a blessing.

You don't realize you are being transformed daily for good or for evil. Embrace that!

Sometimes, we enter into spiritual warfare without realizing it.

Angels are patient. They will wait for you.

You might not recognize that you have been visited by an angel. Ponder that!

Angels help you find things.

Chapter 10

Angels give us ways to escape!

As a believer in Jesus, you have power over ALL the power of the enemy!

Unbelievers avoid your angels.

Chapter 11

There are ranks among the angels! Good or Bad!

There is a Divine Counsel in Heaven made up of angels!

YHVH is the supreme God who judges other gods!

Liars stick together.

The Divine Counsel makes decrees, and they execute what is written.

Pay attention to the true character of a person who claims to be your friend!

This Divine Counsel from heaven directly interacts with humans on earth.

It is possible for an evil spirit to be sent from God.

God knows the end from the beginning in your life

You will judge angels!

Chapter 12

The demise of an evil ruler is settled in Heaven before it manifests on Earth!

Believing the nightly news could cost you your life!

You can reverse the curse! (Repeat)

The elite can be easily terrified, it only takes one dream from God!

God sends angels to deal with National leaders! More often than we realize.

Sometimes, moving in the supernatural will leave you speechless!

The sin of pride aligns you with the devil!

Pay attention: Someone unseen is in your midst.

You have been sealed by God!

Chapter 13

It is the one who finishes the race that receives the prize!

Some people are no longer part of your life for your own protection

Humility often leads to victory!

Satan does not own the earth!

Obedience makes your way prosperous!

We are commanded to be courageous!

You are the Ark of the New Testament!

We don't always recognize that our surroundings are Holy!

God will instill fear in your enemy!

Angels accompany the blast of the shofar! *

When you have an angelic encounter, I would love to add your story to the next volume. Please email me at:

sharoncluck@mindofmessiah.com

If you have been blessed or encouraged by this book, please consider going to Amazon.com and leaving a review. It would be greatly appreciated.

Other books by Sharon M. Cluck

Letting Them Go, Trusting God to Catch them

Angels At War Volume 2

Made in the USA
Monee, IL
09 April 2025

15478047R30142